普通高等教育"十二五"高职高专规划教材

Practical English Writing

新编实用英语

写作（下册）

主　编　肖付良　高　平　刘　燕

副主编　曹淑萍　姚　娟

编　委　（以姓氏笔画为序）

罗凌萍　赵熹妮　胡雁群

黄　珍　龚文锋　谢　丹

中国人民大学出版社
·北京·

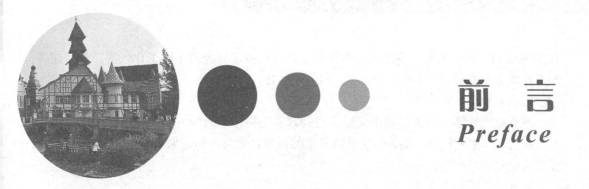

前 言
Preface

　　本教材以一名高职院校毕业生求职应聘涉外文员、涉外商务助理至成长为外贸业务员等涉外商务从业人员的工作过程为主线，以其职业成长过程中所需的典型工作任务为主要内容，以培养涉外商务岗位就业所需的职业能力为目的进行编写。包括《新编实用英语写作（上册）》、《新编实用英语写作（下册）》两册。

　　本书为《新编实用英语写作（下册）》，共需约 64 学时。

一、编写原则

1. 创新性原则

　　以"工作过程导向"为设计理念，教学内容与涉外商务岗位的主要工作过程始终紧密相连，注重涉外商务岗位实际所需的综合职业能力的培养，消除大部分传统写作教材只偏重知识体系的弊端，设计理念创新。

2. 职业性原则

　　广泛调研涉外商务行业，解构职业岗位，选取、整合、序化涉外商务岗位真实工作过程中的典型工作任务，一项典型工作任务为一个主题单元，每个单元又包括若干微工作任务，学习任务与工作任务有机融合，注重职业性。

3. 实用性原则

　　选择涉外商务活动中真实语料作为教学材料，营造真实的语境，既有利于提高英语写作水平，又有利于培养涉外商务职业素质，针对性、实用性强。

4. 多维性原则

　　配备教师用书、教学课件及网络资源，提供合理的教学建议与丰富的辅助资源，方便教师备课与授课，教学资源多维度。

二、教材特色

1. 教学理念注重创新

　　本教材以"工作过程导向"的教育理念为指导，将教学内容及教学过程与岗位工作过程紧密联系、商务英语写作学习与涉外商务岗位职业素质培养有机融合，从而提高英语写作技能及涉外商务职业素质，达到零距离就业的目的，真正体现职业性与应用性。

2. 教学设计注重职业

　　本教材在广泛调研涉外行业、企业的基础上确定编写方案，根据涉外商务岗位职业能力的要求，选取真实工作过程中的典型工作任务，并将其整合、序化为教学内容。设计主题单元，每单元为一项典型工作任务，每项任务又分为若干微工作任务，学习任务与工作任务有机融合，实现"教、学、做"一体化。

3. 选材内容注重实用

本教材选择涉外商务活动中实际应用的真实语料作为教学材料，注重时代性与实用性。真实工作中的选材，能为学生营造真实的语境；学习内容与未来工作内容有机融合，能有效激发学习兴趣。

4. 教学资源注重多维

本教材根据教学需要，配备教师用书、教学课件、网络资源，提供合理的教学建议与丰富的辅助资源，以多维度的教学资源库方便教师备课与授课。

三、教学内容

本册以从事涉外商务岗位所需的典型工作任务为框架，包括建立业务关系，询盘、报盘和还盘，交易达成，支付方式洽谈，装运与保险，申诉与索赔六项典型工作任务。每项典型工作任务由不同的微任务组成，这些微任务又共同组成一个完整的微工作过程。具体分为 6 个主题单元，共 16 课，即建立业务关系（进口商自我介绍、出口商自我介绍）、询盘、报盘、还盘（一般询盘、具体询盘、报盘、还盘），交易达成（订购、寄送合同），支付方式洽谈（支付方式的洽谈、信用证的开立与修改），装运与保险（包装、装运、保险），申诉与索赔（申诉、索赔）。其中一个主题单元即一项典型工作任务，一课即一项微工作任务，每课分为六个模块。各模块由易到难，循序渐进，环环相扣，有机融合典型工作任务与学习任务，让学生完成与工作任务相结合的学习任务，切实提高外贸函电拟写能力和外贸业务实操能力。

模块一　Objectives

明确每课所要掌握的总学习目标，主要包括知识目标、技能目标。

模块二　Writing Tips

介绍每课主题写作的相关知识，让学生了解其构成要素、写作要点、写作技巧等。

模块三　Warm-up Activities

通过图片展示、小组讨论、回答问题、表达看法等多种形式完成与主题单元相关的任务，激发学生对主题单元学习的兴趣，构架联系新旧知识的桥梁，达到激活学生思维、活跃课堂气氛的目的。

模块四　Sample Study

包括 Sample、Vocabulary、Notes、Expressions 等，通过典型样例学习完成主题单元微工作任务所需的主要词汇、表达法、写作格式与技巧等，掌握主题写作的相关知识及技能。

模块五　Practical Writing

根据与课文主题相关的工作任务设计练习，由 Main Information、Key Phrases、Useful Expressions、Letter Writing 构成。Main Information 通过填空练习，学会提炼样例主要信息点，从而了解完成主题单元微工作任务的主要构成要素。Key Phrases、Useful Expressions 通过翻译短语、选词填空、完成句子、改写等多种练习，熟练掌握主题单元写作的主要相关词汇、表达法。Letter Writing 通过完成短文、情景拟写、翻译等练习，熟练拟写格式规范、内容准确的外贸函电。

模块六　Supplementary Reading

本部分遴选紧扣单元主题的补充阅读材料，是课内学习的延展及有益补充。

四、编写队伍

本册各编委为来自湖南娄底职业技术学院、内蒙古河套学院、湖南信息职业技术学院、湘潭职业技术学院等多所高等院校教学经验丰富的一线专业教师，主编为肖付良、高平、刘燕，肖付良负责全书的总纂、终审，副主编为曹淑萍、姚娟，参与编写的其他编委包括罗凌萍、赵熹妮、胡雁群、黄珍、龚文锋、谢丹。外籍专家 Ramon Battershall 先生也参与了本册的审稿工作。我们在调研及编写过程中，得到了诸多行业专家、学者的帮助，在此深表感谢。

鉴于编者水平有限，疏漏在所难免，诚请各位使用者对教材的不足之处提出宝贵意见 (ldxfl@126.com)，以便我们今后修正完善。

编者

2013 年 3 月

目 录
Contents

Contents

Unit 1

Establishing a Business Relationship

Importer's Self-introduction

Objectives

To be proficient in

◎ understanding the main information and key terms often used in a letter of importer's self-introduction

◎ writing a letter of importer's self-introduction

Writing Tips

A letter of importer's self-introduction should be based on equality and mutual benefits. Through self-introduction, the importer makes others know about his information, thus gets more opportunities for achieving potential deals.

Here are some guidelines:

● The tone should be sincere and friendly;

● The offered information should be rich and credible;

● Grammatical errors should be avoided.

Part I
Warm-up Activities

◆ **Write out the common communication methods in the international trade shown in the following pictures.**

◆ **Discuss in groups and give more communication methods in the international trade.**

Part II
Sample Study

Sample 1

October 23, 2011
Haier Group, Haier Industrial Zone
Qingdao, China 266072

Dear Sir or Madam,

We learned about you on the Internet and shall be pleased to *establish* a business relationship with your firm.

We are one of the *leading* importers of electrical goods in Congo and have been for many years. At present we are interested in your refrigerators, details as per our *Enquiry* Note No. 1345 *attached*, and will be glad to receive your *quotation* as soon as possible.

We would like to mention that if your price is attractive and the delivery date acceptable, we shall place an order with you immediately.

Your prompt response will be highly appreciated.

Yours sincerely,
Alexander Co. Ltd.
Jefferson Clinton
Jefferson Clinton
Sales manager

Sample 2

Dear Sir or Madam,

Thank you for your letter of October 23. We desire to enter into a business relationship with your company.

Our refrigerator industry specializes in designing and producing a variety of traditional but fashionable refrigerators. We have developed and marketed new products, such as children's refrigerators and color refrigerators. We can satisfy market needs both at home and abroad. *In compliance with* your request, we are sending you, *under separate cover*, our latest catalogue and price list covering the *export range available* at present.

Should you be interested in any of the items, please let us now. We look forward to your enquiry.

Yours sincerely,

Vocabulary

establish	/ɪs'tæblɪʃ/	v. 建立，成立
leading	/'liːdɪŋ/	a. 重要的，主要的
enquiry	/ɪn'kwaɪərɪ/	n./v. 询价；询问，打听
attached	/ə'tætʃt/	a. 归属的；附属的
quotation	/kwəu'teɪʃn/	n. 报价；时价；行情
available	/ə'veɪləbl/	a. 可用的；可得的
in compliance with		顺从；遵照
under separate cover		另附；另函寄上
export range		出口范围

Notes

1. establish: enter into, set up, forge

establish a business relationship with　　与……建立业务关系

Our company has established a long-term business relationship with yours.

我公司已与贵公司建立了长久的业务关系。

We have established diplomatic relationship with many countries.

我们和许多国家建立了外交关系。

He could not enter into another business arrangement.

他不能开始另一项业务安排。

It's time for us to enter into business negotiation.

到了我们开始谈生意的时间了。

I entered into a partnership with him to do export business.

我与他合伙做出口生意。

2. attached

attached table	附加表；附表
documents attached	备承兑单据；附凭单；附有凭证
attached sheet	附表；附页
attached file	附加文件

I got a no strings attached loan of £3,000.

我得到了一笔3 000英镑的贷款，无任何附加条件。

Talking is not a bad start, so long as the right conditions are attached.

毋庸置疑，只要我们在谈判中提出适当的条件，和谈是一个很好的开始。

3. in compliance with: in agreement/in line/in conformity/ with

in full compliance with	完全遵照
duly in compliance with	完全符合
in compliance with standards	达标准
act in compliance with instructions	遵命办理
in compliance to your request	谨遵要求

This way both parties confirm that the documents that will accompany the draft will constitute evidence of shipment in compliance with the terms of the contract.

那样当事人双方都会确认配合签约条件而附上汇票和证明装船的单据。

Performs is in compliance with company safety standards.

维护过程应完全符合公司的安全标准。

Ensure staff act in compliance with company policies and procedures.

确保员工遵守公司规定和操作流程。

In general, our quotation is in compliance with the present level.

总的说来，我方报价符合当前市场价格水平。

In many cases of complaint, consumers said that what they received are not in compliance with the sample.

在许多投诉案例中，消费者都反映货到后与样品不相符。

4. range 范围

in range with　　　　　　　和……并列

within range of　　　　　　在……范围以内

It's a very broad and free flowing range in our business.

我们的贸易范围非常广泛和自由。

We could not obtain the range list of the heating devices.

我们无法获得有效范围内的取暖设备列表。

 Expressions

For self-introduction

1. We're very experienced in the import of…

2. We wish to introduce ourselves as one of the heading importers of…

3. We have the pleasure to introduce ourselves to you in the hope…

4. Our business line is…

For source of information

1. We got your name and address from the Commercial Counselor's Office of …Embassy in…

2. Your name and address has been passed on to us by…

3. We obtained your name and address from…

4. On the recommendation of…, we know that…

For intention to establish a business relationship

1. We're writing to you in the hope of establishing a business relationship with you.

2. We're writing to you in the hope that we can establish a business relationship with you.

3. We hope to establish a business relationship with you.

4. We hope you can establish a business relationship with us.

For expectation

1. We are looking forward to your early reply.

2. Your prompt response will be highly appreciated.

3. We trust that you will reply to us soon.

4. Looking forward to your favorable reply.

Part III Practical Writing

Main Information

♣ Practice 1

Complete the following chart according to Sample 1.

Source of information: _____

Importer: _____

Intention: _____

Requirements: _____

Key Phrases

♣ Practice 2

Translate the following phrases into Chinese or English.

English	Chinese
desire large capital	_____
latest catalogue	_____
credit standing/ financial standing	_____
export range	_____
specific enquiries	_____
_____	扩大经营范围
_____	建立业务关系
_____	满足不同市场需求
_____	向某人定购
_____	另寄；另邮

♣ Practice 3

Complete the following sentences with the proper form of the words or phrases given in the box.

desire	comply	cover	order	competitive
establish	appreciate	international	extend	hope

1. We're writing to you in the _____ that you can quote us the lowest price.

2. We hope to _____ a business relationship with you early.

3. The color and design of your goods would be highly _____.

4. There is severe competition in the _____ market.

5. We are _____ 100 pieces of printed shirting from you.

6. The quality of our goods can _____ with that of other products.

7. We are sending you a check _____ the first shipment.

8. We are _____ of doing long-term business with you.

9. We are in _____ with your request and will give you the lowest price.

10. KFC achieved in an _____ of its business activities to many countries in Asia.

Useful Expressions

♣ Practice 4

Complete the following sentences in English.

1. We are interested in 和你公司建立友好业务关系. (establish a business relationship)

   知晓你公司是最大的电风扇进口商. (leading)

2. We will be pleased to 马上收到你方最新价目表. (latest pricelist)

   收到你方的长期订单. (regular order)

3. We look forward to 早日收到你方回复. (prompt response)

   你方就交货日期的回复. (delivery)

♣ Practice 5

Rewrite the underlined parts in the letter below with two different expressions, but without changing the meaning of the sentences.

Dear Sir,

　　①We obtained your name and address from Mr. Smith, who has done business with us for many years.

　　②We have been the leading importer of jumpers for 15 years, and are planning to extend our business in our neighboring countries. We have received many enquiries for jumpers from the clients. ③We are considering the possibility of establishing a business relationship with you if this is possible.

　　④Your prompt response shall be appreciated.

Yours faithfully,

① We obtained your name and address from Mr. Smith

a. _____

b. _____

② We have been the leading importer of jumpers for 15 years

a. _____

b. _____

③ We are considering the possibility of establishing a business relationship with you

a. _____

b. _____

④ Your prompt response shall be appreciated

a. _____

b. _____

Letter Writing

♣ Practice 6

Compose a letter of importer's self-introduction with the given information.

① We have been one of the leading importers of casual shoes for many years

② Attention: Mr. Li Xiang, Sales Department

③ detailed specification as per the attached illustration

④ Would you like to have a look at it

⑤ you are interested in establishing a business relationship with us

August 20, 2011

Jinjiang Shoes Import & Export Corporation

6 East Xindai Street, Qingyang Town, Jinjiang

Fujian, China

_____

Dear Sirs,

　　We learn about you from Fort & Co. Ltd., and we are writing in the hope that _____.

　　_____. At present we are in need of women's leather shoes for a quantity of 1,000, _____. We can make 20% down payment and grant you 3% commission. _____ and subsequently inform us if you can supply?

　　We look forward to your early reply.

Yours faithfully,

♣ Practice 7

Write a letter of importer's self-introduction according to the information given below.

　　You are an importer of electrical goods in the US. Recently, you got a piece of information about the air-conditioners produced by Gree Company in China from the Internet. You are interested in their products. Now you write a letter to them, hoping to establish a business relationship.

Practice 8

Complete the letter according to the Chinese in the parentheses.

Dear Sir or Madam,

Thank you for your letter dated December 3. We desire to enter into a business relationship with you.

Our company design and produce various fashionable cotton slippers. ① _____ (我们已开发和上市了新产品), such as casual slippers, embroidery slippers. ② _____ (我们能满足国内外市场需求).

③ _____ (随函附寄最新的产品目录及价目表). If you are interested in any of the items, please let us know. Your prompt response will be highly appreciated.

Yours sincerely,

Part Ⅳ
Supplementary Reading

Reading One

Dear Sir or Madam,

At the start of this month, we attended the Harrogate Toy Fair. While there, we had an interesting conversation with Mr. Douglas Gage of Edutoys PLC about selecting an agency for our teaching aids. Douglas described your dynamic sales force and innovative approach to marketing. He attributed his company's success to your excellent distribution network which has served him for several years. We need an organization like yours to launch our products in the UK.

Our teaching aids cover the whole range of primary education in all subjects. Our patented Matrix math apparatus is particularly successful. We enclose an illustrated catalogue of our British English editions for your information.

We shall be in London during the first two weeks of October. Perhaps we could arrange a meeting to discuss the proposal.

Yours sincerely,

Reading Two

Dear Sir or Madam,

Thank you for your letter of 12 April proposing a sole agency for our office machines. In view of our long and mutually beneficial collaboration, we would be very pleased to entrust you with the sole agency for Bahrain.

From our records, we are pleased to note that you have two service engineers who took training courses at our Milan factory. The sole agency will naturally maintain your training qualified after-sales staff.

We have drawn up a draft agreement that is enclosed. Please examine the detailed terms and conditions and let us know whether they meet with your approval.

Yours sincerely,

Exporter's Self-introduction

Objectives

To be proficient in

◎ understanding the main information and key terms used in a letter of exporter's self-introduction

◎ writing a letter of exporter's self-introduction

Writing Tips

In order to write a proper exporter's self-introduction letter, some guidelines should be followed:

● stating the source of information briefly;

● making a brief, not a long introduction to the exporter's products or services, the main strengths etc.;

● showing the writing intention clearly;

● giving more information and expressing the expectation of an early reply.

Part I Warm-up Activities

◆ Discuss in pairs and write out the company names according to the pictures shown below.

◆ **Work in pairs and tell more information about the companies above.**

Part II
Sample Study

Sample 1

August 16, 2011
Pella Co., Ltd.
20 Newell Street
London, Britain
Dear Sir or Madam,

We *owe* your name and address *to* the *Commercial Counselor's Office* of the Italian *Embassy* in Beijing who has informed us that you are in the market for Chinese *porcelain*. We *avail* ourselves of this opportunity to approach you for the establishment of trade relationship with you.

We are a well-known brand company, mainly *handling* the export of Chinese porcelain. And we have exported Chinese porcelain for more than 40 years.

Our company has enjoyed good *reputation in this line*. In order to *acquaint* you with our business lines, we enclose a copy of our export list covering the main items available at present.

Should any of the items be of interest to you, please let us know. We shall be glad to give you our quotation *upon receipt of* your detailed requirements. It is our hope to promote, by joint efforts, a trade relationship to our *mutual* advantage.

We look forward to receiving your enquiries soon.
Yours sincerely,
Jiangxi Porcelain Import & Export Corporation
28 Xinping Road, Jingdezheng, Jiangxi, China
Sally Wang
Sally Wang
Sales manager

Sample 2

August 22, 2011

Dear Sally Wang,

Thanks for your letter of August 16 and the export list *attached*.

We are very interested in your Chinese porcelain of Article No.1806, 1812 and 1819. And we are ready to place a trial order with you. Please mail us the detailed information about FOB China port, terms of payment and earliest delivery date.

If we find your price is competitive and the delivery date is acceptable, we are willing to place a large order and establish a long relationship with you.

Yours sincerely,

Michael Jackson

Michael Jackson

Marketing Manager

Vocabulary

embassy	/'embəsɪ/	*n.* 大使馆；大使馆全体成员
avail	/ə'veɪl/	*v.* 有利于；有助于　*n.* 益处
porcelain	/'pɔːslɪn/	*n.* 瓷；瓷器
handle	/'hændl/	*v.* 处理；应付，对待
reputation	/ˌrepju'teɪʃən/	*n.* 名气，名声；名誉
acquaint	/ə'kweɪnt/	*v.* 使认识，使了解；使熟悉
mutual	/'mjutʃʊəl/	*a.* 相互的，彼此的；共同的
attach	/ə'tætʃ/	*v.* 连接；使附属
owe…to…		由于，归功于
Commercial Counselor's Office		商务参赞处
in this line		在本行业
upon receipt of		一收到

Notes

1. handle　　carry on; deal with

I was impressed by her handling of the affair.

我觉得她对此事的处理很了不起。

Most customers were satisfied with the way their complaints were handled.

绝大多数的客户对他们的投诉被处理的方式感到满意。

2. line   department of activity; type of business   行业；业务

Our company has been engaged for many years in the line of household appliances.

我们从事家用电器业务已有多年。

You know our price is lower than the ones of the same line.

我们的价格是同类产品中比较低的。

3. joint   连接的；共同的，联合的

joint venture 合资企业

joint management 联营

joint purchase 联购

joint sales 联销

by joint efforts   通过共同努力

By our joint efforts, we managed to complete the project on time.

我们通过共同努力总算按时完成了计划。

In order to achieve this goal, we will strengthen our cooperation and make joint efforts.

为了达到这个目标，我们将加强合作，共同努力。

4. upon receipt of

Upon receipt of your payment, we'll ship the goods by air.

一收到你方货款，我们即空运此货。

Upon receipt of any such notice, customer may terminate this agreement on the expiration date.

客户接到通知后，可以在终止日期终止合同。

Expressions

For self-introduction

1. We write to introduce ourselves to you as one of the largest exporters from…

2. We wish to introduce ourselves as one of the leading exporters of…

3. We are one of the largest … in our country and have handled with the products for…

4. We are specializing in …

For source of information

1. We owe your name and address to the Commercial Counselor's Office of … Embassy in…

2. Your firm has been recommended to us by…, with whom we have done business for…

3. Through the courtesy of … we come to know your name and address.

4. We have learned, from…, that you are a leading importer of …, and at present you are in the market for electric fans.

For intention to establishing business relationship

1. We approach you today in the hope of establishing a business relationship with you and expect, by our joint effect, to enlarge our business scope.

2. In order to acquaint you with our business lines, we enclose a copy of our illustrated catalogue covering the main items available at present.

3. If you are interested in any of the items, please tell us by fax.

4. As this item falls within the scope of our business activities, we shall be pleased to enter into a business relationship with you.

Part III
Practical Writing

Main Information

♣ Practice 1

Complete the following chart according to Sample 1.

Source of information: _____

Exporter: _____

Self-introduction: _____

Intention: _____

Requirements: _____

Key Phrases

♣ Practice 2

Translate the following phrases into Chinese or English.

English	Chinese
through the courtesy of Mr. Black	_____
be given to understand/get to know/be informed that	_____
fall within/lie within /belong to	_____
give you a general/rough idea of	_____
be in line of toys	_____
_____	随函附上一份目录
_____	一份介绍我方业务范围的清单
_____	供应短缺
_____	与意大利的客户有很多联系
_____	得到我们最认真和及时的关注

♣ Practice 3

Complete the following sentences with the proper form of the words or phrases given in the box.

specialize	through the courtesy of	be in short supply	enclose	demand
in this line	know	catalogue	a wide range of	a general idea of

1. Specializing in the export of Chinese cotton piece goods, we express our desire to trade with you _____ .

2. Our company is _____ for exporting our silk in good quality with different styles and colors in North America.

3. Our company _____ in machinery featured by its light weight, high precision and simple operation.

4. To give you a general idea of our products, we _____ herewith our Price List No. TP118/2860 with details for your reference.

5. _____ the Commercial Counselor's Office of the Canadian Embassy in Beijing informing us that you are in the market for Chinese green tea.

6. Because of very wet spring weather, apples will _____ this year.

7. We are enclosing a copy of our recent _____ with a few samples which may possibly interest you, and shall be glad to hear from you at any time.

8. Here are the catalogue, pattern books. Perhaps they'll give you _____ our products.

9. We write to introduce ourselves as one of the largest exporters, from China, of _____ machinery and equipments.

10. We have learnt that there is a good _____ for walnut meat in your market, and take this opportunity of enclosing our Quotation Sheet No. 328 for your consideration.

Useful Expressions

♣ Practice 4

Complete the following sentences in English.

1. We send you a new catalogue to give you a general idea of 出口绿茶 .

   主要出口产品 .

   经营产品范围 .

2. 承蒙上海工商会的推荐，we are pleased to understand you are a well-known importer of Chinese porcelain in your area.

   承蒙 Black Andrew 先生的引荐，we are given to understand that you are one of the leading importers of machinery products in France.

   从商务参赞处获悉，we take the pleasure of knowing that you are going to import some art and craft products from China.

3. We will be pleased to inform you that the commodities you are interested in 属于我们的经营范围 .

We are pleased to know that you are the leading manufactures and 家用电器产品的进口商 .

We take the pleasure to inform you that 邮寄上一份涵盖我方经营商品的价目表 .

❖ Practice 5

Rewrite the underlined parts in the letter below with two different expressions, but without changing the meaning of the sentences.

Dear Sirs,

①We have learned from Alibaba website that ②you want to purchase small household appliances.

Taking this opportunity we would like to introduce you our company (Bronton services LTD). ③We have been the leading exporter of small household appliances for 26 years, and are planning to extend our business to our neighboring countries.

④We provide you the high quality services and the reasonable prices. We enclose a copy of latest catalog covering the detailed items available, and hope you will have interest to them.

Your reply is awaited with much interest.

Yours faithfully,

Black Small Household Appliances Co. Ltd.

Andrew Black

Andrew Black

① We have learned from

a. _____

b. _____

② you want to purchase small household appliances

a. _____

b. _____

③ We have been the leading exporter of small household appliances

a. _____

b. _____

④ We provide you the high quality service and the reasonable prices

a. _____

b. _____

Letter Writing

🍀 **Practice 6**

Compose a reply letter of the above exporter's self-introduction with the information given below.

① together with your bank credit and advantages in price and regular supplies

② Please quote us the best price CIF Huston

③ if the goods are of good quality and a reasonable price

④ securing large orders for you

⑤ We are showing so great interest in your small household appliances item No. 299

January 12, 2011

Dear Andrew Black,

    Thanks for your letter of January 12. _____.

_____.

    We are confident of _____ and we are taking the great pleasure of establishing a trade business relationship _____. Please send us some general idea of your lines _____.

    Your favourable reply would be highly appreciated.

Yours sincerely,

Alexander Co. Ltd.

Jafferson Clinton

Jafferson Clinton

🍀 **Practice 7**

Write a letter of exporter's self-introduction according to the information below.

    You are Williams PT Company in Britain, an exporter manufacturing computer products. Recently you got a piece of information from the Commercial Counselor's Office of your embassy in Beijing that Xinxin Trade Company is the leading personal computer importer in China. Now you write a letter to them by introducing your company and your products.

🍀 **Practice 8**

Complete the reply to the letter of Practice 7 according to the Chinese in the parentheses.

Dear Mr. Williams,

    Thank you for your letter of June 22. ①_____ (我们对贵公司的电脑产品非常感兴趣) that we are confident of ②_____ (和贵公司有大量的订单)

and ③_____ (我们很高兴建立业务关系) with your corporation. Please let us get some general idea of your lines with your bank credit and advantages in price and regular supplies.

④_____ (我们将不胜感激) if you could send us quotation and sample books.

Your favorable reply would be highly appreciated.

Yours sincerely,

Part IV
Supplementary Reading

Reading One

20 July, 2011

Mr. Steven Clark

Marketing Head,

SP Trade Corporation

102 East Street

Arizona, California,

USA

Dear Mr. Steven Clark,

We have had your name and address from China Council for the Promotion of International Trade that you are in the market for homecare product and are now writing you hoping to enter into a business relationship with you. Being in these lines for over thirty years, you can be assured of the best quality and reasonable price.

At present, we have produced the newest vacuum cleaner designed for cleaning the dirty corners of house roof edges, the series of vacuum clearer own the characteristics of being light, power efficient and durable. You will find details in the catalogue attached. If you have any interest in dealing in our products, don't hesitate to contact us.

Your early reply will be highly appreciated.

Yours sincerely,

Andrew Freeman

Andrew Freeman

Sales manager

Reading Two

Dear Sirs,

Through the courtesy of Mr. Robert Smith, we have learned that you are in the market of health care products.

We are taking pleasure in informing you that we are an exporter dealing a variety of health care products. Recently we have developed a series of new products of the best quality and caring function. Enclosed please find a copy of the catalogue.

If you have any interest in our products, please contact us.

We look forward to cooperating with you.

Yours sincerely,

Unit 2

Enquiry, Offer and Counter-offer

General Enquiries

Objectives

To be proficient in

◎ understanding all the main information and key terms often used in a letter of general enquiry

◎ writing a letter of general enquiry

Writing Tips

An enquiry is usually made by a buyer without engagement to get information for goods or services they are interested in. Enquiries may fall into two categories: general enquiries (一般询盘) and specific enquiries (具体询盘). If an importer wants to get a general idea of the business scope of the exporter, he may make a request for a pricelist, a catalogue, samples and so forth. This is called a general enquiry. Generally, it is also a first enquiry.

This enquiry is not intended to conclude a specific transaction immediately. Usually, the buyer will enquire about different sellers simultaneously for the same commodity as comparison to get the competitive price. A letter of general enquiry should be written concisely, clearly and to the point.

Here are some guidelines:

When enquiring, you should

● give the source of information and make a brief self-introduction;

● express the intention of writing the letter;

● state the possibility of placing an order.

When replying, you should

● express thanks for the enquiry;

● give a full answer to the enquiry;

● write in a sincere and friendly tone and end your letter by hoping receiving specific enquiry.

Part I
Warm-up Activities

◆ Write out the four steps involved in the business negotiation after discussing with your partner.

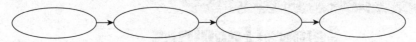

◆ Give some aims of a general enquiry.

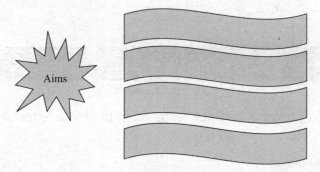

Aims

Part II
Sample Study

Sample 1

October 15, 2011

Dear Sir or Madam,

    We were informed from Brother Co. that you are the leading exporter of cotton bed sheets and quilt covers in your country. We are taking this opportunity to approach you in the hope of establishing a business relationship with you.

    We'd like to *request* that you send us your latest catalogue and price list at your earliest convenience.

    We happen to be the largest *distributor* in textiles located in Guangzhou, China. Having been in this line of business for many years, we believe there is a *promising* market between us.

    Should your price be found *competitive* and your goods up to standard, we intend to place a large order with you immediately.

Yours sincerely,

Sample 2

Dear Sirs,

Thank you for your enquiry of October 15. We are pleased to learn that you are interested in our commodities.

Enclosed you can find our latest catalogues and a price list regarding the details you ask for. We are also sending you, under separate cover, some samples which will show you clearly our excellent quality and skilled *workmanship*. We are sure you will agree that our products are both excellent in quality and reasonable in price.

We offer a 3% discount for a bulk purchase of up to 10,000 pieces. As for terms of payment, it is our custom to trade on the basis of a confirmed and irrevocable letter of credit.

Thanks again for your interest in our products. Should you be interested in any items, please let us know. We are looking forward to your further enquiries.

Yours sincerely,

Vocabulary

request	/rɪ'kwest/	n./v. 要求；请求
distributor	/dɪ'strɪbjətə/	n. 经销商，发货者
promising	/'prɒmɪsɪŋ/	a. 有前途的
competitive	/kəm'petətɪv/	a. 竞争力强的
enclose	/ɪn'kləʊz/	v. 随信附寄
workmanship	/'wɜːkmənʃɪp/	n. 手艺，技能；工艺品

Notes

1. enquiry (or inquiry)

make (or: send, give, fax) sb. an enquiry for sth.

向某人询购某种商品 / 向某人询问某种商品的价格

They send us an enquiry for our "Cool" Brand Air Conditioner.

他们来信询购"凉爽"牌空调。

Thank you for your enquiry of August 1 for 3,000 m/t Dongbei Rice.

感谢你方 8 月 1 日有关 3 000 公吨东北大米的询盘。

to enquire for   对……询价

enquire for digital cameras   对数码相机的询价

The goods you enquire for are out of stock.

所询之货已脱销。

She inquired after/ about the new catalogue in the shopping mall.

她向购物中心索要了新的目录。

enquire about 打听或询问某人或某事的情况

We are writing to you to enquire about the current price of high quality gloves.

我们特写信询问有关优质手套的时价。

其他相关词组：

to make an enquiry	发出询盘；向……询价
enquiry sheet	询价单
general enquiry	一般询盘
specific enquiry	具体询盘
an occasional enquiry	偶尔询盘
keep enquiry in mind	记住询盘

2. intend to 打算，想要干什么

Do you really intend to close with his offer?

你真的打算接受他的开价？

Today, I intend to book the shipment space.

今天我打算去订舱。

When do you intend to give the invitation?

贵方打算什么时候招标呢？

3. place an order with sb. for sth. 向某人订购某物

order   n. 订单

名词 order 常与动词 make, send, place 等连用，如果表示订购某项货物，后接介词 for/on/of。

If your price is in line with market price, we will send you an order for 5,000 sets.

如果你方价格与市价相符，我们将定购 5 000 台。

If your price is reasonable, we may place a large order with you.

若你方价格合理，我们可能向你大量订购。

order   v. 订购，订（货）

If you allow us 10% discount, we will order 10,000 dozen.

如果你方给予 10% 的折扣，我们将订购 10 000 打。

4. enclosed

Enclosed are some samples.

随函附寄一些样品。

Please complete and return the enclosed questionnaire.

所附问卷请填妥交回。

Enclosed a draft for $300, 000 which was drawn on by our London house.

同函奉上伦敦分公司向贵公司开出面额 300 000 美元的汇票一张。

A check for ten pounds is enclosed.

附上一张十英镑的支票。

Please fill in the form enclosed herewith.

请填写随函附上之表格。

Enclosed please find a money order.

兹附上一张汇票，请查收。

5. discount   *n.* 折扣

allow/give/make/grant…% discount off/on the prices of goods

按货价给予……% 的折扣

cash discount	现金折扣
quantity discount	数量折扣
special discount	特别折扣

We give a 10% discount for cash payment.

现金付款，我们给予九折优惠。

We are prepared to allow you a special discount of 5% to compensate for the trouble caused.

我们准备给予你方 5% 的特别折扣，以补偿给你方造成的不便。

The highest discount we can offer you on this item is 10%.

这种商品我们所能给的最高折扣是 10%。

To be frank, a discount of 5% will not help very much.

坦率地说，5% 的折扣意义不大。

6. as to 关于，至于

As to terms of payment, we require L/C.

关于付款，我们要求用信用证。

As to the samples, we'll send them to you under separate cover as soon as possible.

至于样品，我们将尽快另寄给你方。

As to payment terms, it is our custom to trade on the basis of a confirmed and irrevocable letter of credit.

有关付款方式，我们贸易的一贯做法是采用保兑的不可撤销的信用证。

 Expressions

For reasons of enquiry

1. We can now take advantage of /avail ourselves of this opportunity to write to you with a

view to/in the hope of entering into a business relationship with you.

2. We are writing to express our desire to establish/enter into/open up/set up/build up business relations/business connections with your firm.

3. We specialize in … and are willing to establish a business relationship with you/and we wish to deal with you in this line.

4. We are now writing you for the purpose of establishing a business relationship with you.

For asking the basic business scope of the addressee

1. Please send us full details about your products.

2. We would appreciate receiving details regarding samples.

3. I should be grateful if you send me your business terms including catalogues, pricelist etc.

4. Please let us know your terms of business.

For asking for price

1. Kindly quote us your lowest prices for...

2. Please quote your best/most competitive/lowest price.

3. Please quote your price/FOB/CIF…

4. We are desirous of having your lowest price for...

For giving references

1. Information about our company can be found in/at...

2. For information about our company please refer to/contact...

3. Should you wish to make any enquiries about us, please write to...

4. We shall be pleased to provide the usual trade references.

For wishing further business

1. If the goods come up to our expectation, we would expect to place regular orders.

2. If the samples meet with our approval, we intend to place substantial orders.

3. If your prices are competitive and your goods are up to standard, we shall order on a regular basis.

4. If you can let us have a competitive quotation, we trust business will ensure...

For replying an enquiry

1. We are pleased to receive your enquiry of…and are enclosing our…as requested.

2. We are pleased to know that we have been recommended by…

3. We hope the above information will turn out to be useful to you.

4. Please feel free to contact us again if you have any further questions.

Practical Writing

Main Information

♣ Practice 1

Complete the following chart according to Sample 1.

Source of information: _____

Importer: _____

Intention: _____

Requirements: _____

Key Phrases

♣ Practice 2

Translate the following phrases into Chinese or English.

English	Chinese
in this line of business	_____
in the hope of doing something	_____
at one's earliest convenience	_____
terms of payment	_____
latest catalogue	_____
_____	带有插图的目录
_____	另函附寄
_____	期待，期望
_____	利用
_____	建立业务关系

♣ Practice 3

Complete the following sentences with the proper form of the words or phrases given in the box below.

deliver	enquiry	appeal to	intend to	pay
order	compete	regard	manufacture	catalogue

1. I'm afraid I don't find your price _____ at all.

2. Thank you for your _____ dated November 23rd.

3. As a _____ of computers, we are desirous of entering into a direct business relationship with you.

4. If your prices are favorable, I can place the _____ right away.

5. We are grateful if you can make a prompt _____.

6. Could you please send us a _____ of your rubber boots, together with terms of payment?

7. These are our normal terms of _____ in international business.

8. We would appreciate receiving details _____ the commodities.

9. When do you _____ negotiate the payment terms with the firm?

10. On balance, joint ventures _____ me more than state-owned enterprises.

Useful Expressions

♣ Practice 4

Translate the following sentences into English.
1. 我方从 ABC 公司处得知你公司供应毛衫。
2. 正如你们所知，我们是经营此类商品多年的国有公司。
3. 我们有意获得你方新产品的商品目录及价目单。
4. 如果你方价格具有竞争力并且付款方式可以接受的话，我们打算下一笔大订单。
5. 对成批购买我们给予3个百分点的优惠，凭不可撤销的即期信用证付款。
6. 我们期待和你公司建立长期的互惠互利的合作关系。

♣ Practice 5

Rewrite the underlined parts in the letter below with two different expressions, but without changing the meaning of the sentences.

Dear Sir or Madam,

①We found your name and address from the Internet and we know that you are interested in Telecontrol Racing Car produced in China. Now, ②we are writing to hope that we can establish a business relationship with you.

Our company was founded in 1952, and ③it specializes in toys and handicrafts. We have already become one of the biggest import & export companies in China. Telecontrol Racing Car is our new product, and it is very popular all over the world.

Our products hold a high reputation among the clients throughout the world for their high quality and favorable price.

In order to give you a general idea of various kinds of products that we are handling, we are airmailing you our latest catalogue for reference. ④Please let us know if you are interested in our products.

We look forward to your early reply.

Yours faithfully,

① We found your name and address from the Internet

a. _____

b. _____

② we are writing you to hope that we can establish a business relationship with you

a. _____

b. _____

③ it specializes in toys and handicrafts

a. _____

b. _____

④ Please let us know immediately if you are interested in our products

a. _____

b. _____

Letter Writing

◆ Practice 6

Compose a letter of general enquiry with the given information.

① you are a big exporter of various toys for children

② Attention: Wang Ping, Sales Manager

③ send us a copy of your product catalogue

④ We are looking for a supplier as our long-term partner

⑤ inclusive of our 2% commission

⑥ we will place a large order with you immediately

August 22, 2011

Changsha Children's Toys Import & Export Corporation

6 Xiangfu Street, Changsha, Hunan, China

_____

Dear Sirs,

We understand you from the Internet that _____, such as electric toys, inflatable toys and plush toys. We have been one of the leading importers of toys in our region for many years.

_____. We would like to request you to _____ with the price of one single or sample table, and quote us your lowest price, CIF London, _____.

If your price is favorable and the delivery date is acceptable, _____.

Please give us your reply as soon as possible.

Yours faithfully,

Mark Matthews

Marketing Manager

Practice 7

Write a letter of general enquiry according to the information given below.

You are a dealer in hand-made commodities from Jackson Trading Company, based in Toronto, Canada. Recently you get informed about the hand-made gloves produced by Nanjing Jinling Import & Export Co. Ltd in China on the Internet. You, Joe Brown are interested in their products. Now you write Cathy Liu Cathy@msn.com a letter to make a general enquiry about catalogue, price, payment terms and samples for their gloves.

Practice 8

Complete the reply to the letter of Practice 7 according to the Chinese in the parentheses.

Dear Joe Brown,

Thank you for your letter dated on October 11th. We are pleased to know that you are interested in our products. In fact, ①＿＿＿＿＿＿＿＿＿＿＿＿＿＿＿ (我们很期待与贵方建立贸易关系).

②＿＿＿＿＿＿＿＿＿＿＿＿＿ (谨遵要求，另函奉上), we are sending you a copy of our latest catalogue, together with samples of some of our products.

I regret to say that we cannot send you the full range of samples. You can be assured, however, that all of our products are of the same high quality. Enclosed you can also find our price list covering our present available export range.

As for terms of payment ③＿＿＿＿＿＿＿＿＿＿＿＿＿＿＿ (我们凭即期汇票支付的不可撤销的信用证付款).

Thank you again for your interest in our products. If you would like more information, please let us know as soon as possible. We'll be glad to assist you in any way we can.

Yours faithfully,

Cathy Liu

Part IV
Supplementary Reading

Reading One

September 5, 2011

Dear Sir or Madam,

Wool Quilts

You were recommended to us by the Australian Embassy as one of the leading companies in Australia exporting wool quilts. We are writing to enquire whether you would be willing to establish a business relationship with us.

We have been importers of wool products for many years. At present, we find that there is a growing demand for wool quilts in this market, so we intend to expend our range and we are hoping to be the first to introduce this product in our district.

We would be pleased if you could send us your catalogue, specifications, pricelist together with any samples you can supply. We would also appreciate it if you could tell us the payment practices with which you do business with others. If your prices are competitive, we will expect to transact a significant volume of business.

We look forward to receiving your letter.

Yours sincerely,

Reading Two

September 8, 2011

Dear Sir or Madam,

Re: Wool Quilts

Thank you very much for your enquiry dated September 5 regarding our wool quilts. We shall be glad to enter into a business relationship with your company. As requested, under separate cover, we have air-mailed our latest illustrated catalogue, pricelist and samples covering our export range.

As for terms of payment, it is our custom to trade on the basis of a confirmed and irrevocable letter of credit.

Our wool quilts have enjoyed popularity in the world market for their excellent quality and low price for many years. We are confident that our products will help you expand your market and bring you rich profits.

Should you wish to place an order, please contact us immediately.

Yours sincerely,

Lesson Four •••

Specific Enquiries

Objectives

To be proficient in
◎ understanding the main information and key terms often used in a letter of specific enquiry
◎ writing a letter of specific enquiry

Writing Tips

When an importer wants to purchase certain kind of products, he may ask the exporter to make an offer or a quotation for the goods including such substantive information as the price, specifications, discounts, quantity, terms of payment and date of shipment. That is called a specific enquiry.

When enquiring, you should
● point out what products you need and ask for a quotation or an offer for this item;
● ask specifically what information or service you need the addressee to supply. This may include price, quantity, packing, payment and delivery, etc.;
● state the possibility of placing an order.

When replying, you should
● begin by expressing thanks for the enquiry;
● give a full answer to the enquiry and try to explain if you cannot do as requested;
● end your letter by hoping for business and by offering further help.

Part I
Warm-up Activities

◆ **Write out what you would need to know about in your letter of enquiry.**

send an enquiry

I'd like to know:
_____
_____
_____

◆ **Give more information you need to know about after discussion with your partner.**

Part II
Sample Study

Sample 1

May 23, 2011

Dear Sir or Madam,

This company is one of the major *importers* of knitwear in New York. We were impressed by the selection of sweaters that were displayed on your stand at the *exhibition* held in Chicago last month.

At present, we are in need of men's woolen cardigans and men's woolen pullovers.

We are enclosing our enquiry note and looking forward to receiving your *quotation* soon, C.I.F. New York *inclusive* of our 5% *commission*. When quoting, please also state the earliest date of delivery, terms of payment, and available quantity. We would be most appreciative if you could also provide us with samples in different colors.

If your quotation is competitive, we are ready to conduct substantial business with you.

An early reply will be much appreciated.

Yours faithfully,

Sample 2

May 25, 2011

Dear Sir or Madam,

Thank you very much for your enquiry dated May 23. We are pleased to send you our quotation as requested.

We have a wide range of products, providing men's woolen cardigans and pullovers in *assorted* colors and with all sizes available (XL, L, M and S).

We have a minimum export quantity of 100 dozen per color and can meet orders of over 10,000 dozen at one time. For the item you require, we ask for a price of US$300.00 per dozen, CIFC 5% New York.

We usually arrange our delivery within 25 days after receipt of L/C. As for the terms of payment, we prefer irrevocable L/C at sight. Furthermore, also according to your request, we are sending you by airmail our latest samples in different colors for your reference.

Experience shows many orders will follow in this season and a sharp price rise will be on the way. So, you are *cordially* invited to take advantage of this attractive offer. We trust that our experience in manufacturing these products and our *reliable* quality will win your confidence.

Expecting your first order.

Yours faithfully,

Vocabulary

importer	/ɪmˈpɔːtə/	n. 进口商
exhibition	/ˌeksəˈbɪʃən/	n. 展示，展览
quotation	/kwəʊˈteɪʃən/	n. 报价
inclusive	/ɪnˈklusɪv/	a. 包含……在内的
commission	/kəˈmɪʃən/	n. 佣金; 授权，委托
assorted	/əˈsɔːtɪd/	a. 多样混合的，各种各样的
cordially	/ˈkɔːdjəlɪ/	ad. 深切地；诚挚地
reliable	/rɪˈlaɪəbl/	a. 可靠的，可信的

Notes

1. quotation

make a quotation 报价

make you a quotation for shirts 衬衣报价

quote *v.* 报价

to quote sb. a price for sth.

to quote sb. for sth.

We will be glad to quote you CIF London.

我们将给贵方报 CIF 伦敦价。

We will quote you the lowest price if you send us your specific enquiry.

如提出具体询价，我们将给贵公司报最低价。

Please quote us for 500 dozen of printed aprons.

请给本公司报 500 打印花围裙价。

Please quote us your lowest price CIF Lagos.

请报最低 CIF 拉各斯价。

Will you please quote us for the following items?

请就以下货物报价。

2. CIF = Cost, Insurance & Freight

CIF 即 "成本、保险费加运费（……指定目的港）"，或 "到岸价格"。是指在装运港当货物越过船舷时，卖方即完成交货，卖方必须支付将货物运至指定的目的港所需的运费和费用，但交货后货物灭失或损坏的风险，及由于各种事件造成的任何额外费用，即由卖方转移到买方。但是，在 CIF 条件下卖方还必须办理买方货物在运输途中灭失或损坏风险的海运保险。

CIF Guangzhou, inclusive of our 2% commission.

广州 CIF(到岸价)，含佣金 2%。

The price we offer is calculated on CIF basis.

我公司所报的价是按 CIF(到岸价) 计算的。

Is your price on a FOB or CIF basis?

你方报价是船上交货价还是到岸价 ?

The invoice was for £ 35 CIF.

发票为到岸价 35 英镑。

FOB=Free on Board "船上交货价" 或称 "离岸价格"

FOB 是指货物在指定的装运港越过船舷，卖方即完成交货。这意味着买方必须从该点起承担货物灭失或损坏的一切风险。FOB 术语要求卖方办理货物出口清关手续。

其他常用价格术语：

C&F Cost and Freight   "成本加运费" 或 "离岸加运费" 价

FOR—Free on Rail   火车交货价

FOT—Free on Truck	汽车交货价
FAS—Free Alongside Ship	船边交货价
Ex Factory	工厂交货价
Ex Plantation	农场交货价
Ex Warehouse	仓库交货价
Ex Ship	目的港船上交货价
Ex Dock Duty Paid	目的港码头完税交货价
Ex Dock Duty Unpaid	目的港码头未完税交货价

3. be inclusive of = include

4. commission

佣金是中间商因介绍交易或代买商品而获取的报酬。中间商因其有一定的贸易渠道，因此通过其开展交易已是国际贸易中的一种普遍做法。

Expressions:

all commissions 一切佣金或各项佣金

a commission of ...% / ...% commission 百分之几佣金

two or several items of commission 两笔或几笔佣金

your/our commission of ...%/your/our ...% commission 你方 / 我方百分之几佣金

draw /receive a commission of...% on ... 抽取（收取）……% 的佣金

The above price includes your 2% commission.

以上所开价格包括你方 2% 的佣金。

Please quote ten tons of steels CIF Guangzhou, including 5% commission.

请报十吨钢材广州 CIF(到岸价)，包括 5% 佣金。

5. state 告知

In your quotation, please state the delivery time.

请于报价时告知交货时间。

Please quote us your lowest price CIF New York, stating the terms of payment and the shipment date.

请报你方最低纽约到岸价，并请告知支付方式和装运期。

6. shipment

make/effect shipment 装运

ship   *v.* 装运

When can you make shipment?

什么时候装运?

7. available

commodities available for export 供出口的商品

not available 缺货

The only opportunity available now is the Canton Fair.

目前唯一的机会就是广交会。

We are sending you, under cover, a catalogue covering the goods available at present.

随函附上一份我方目前可供货物的目录单。

There are no such men's shirts available for export.

没有这种男式衬衫可供出口。

Please ship the goods by the first available steamer.

请把货物装上第一班轮船。

Can you quote us a price for your bicycles available for export?

请就可供出口的自行车报价。

8. substantial 大量的

If your price is competitive, we can place a substantial order.

如果价格优惠，我方将大量订货。

9. conclude/ close business with sb. 与某人达成生意

10. appreciate   *v.* 感谢

sb. appreciate sth.

sb. appreciate it if…

sth. be appreciated

We appreciate very much your favorable reply.

非常感谢您的回复。

We shall appreciate it if you will send us a brochure and some of your samples by air immediately.

如能立即给我们航空寄来一本小册子和部分样品，我们将十分感激。

Your early reply is highly appreciated.

如能早日回复，不胜感激。

We highly appreciate your friendly cooperation.

我们十分感激贵公司的合作。

 Expressions

For introductory statements about resources of information or previous letters, etc.

1. We know your company through…

2. We are a company dealing in…

3. We write to inform you that we are interested in…

4. We are glad to note from your letter of… This happen to coincide with our desire.

For reasons of enquiry

1. We're interested in/ take interest in…

2. We need /are in the market for…

3. We have received many enquiries from our customers for…

4. We have a considerable demand here for…

For specific enquiry

1. If you can quote us a firm offer for…we shall appreciate it.

2. We will be pleased to accept your offer…

3. Your quotation for the following will be highly appreciated.

4. Full information as to prices, quality, quantity available and other relative information would be appreciated.

5. We would be obliged if you would give us a quotation…

For wishing to cooperate

1. We would like very much to cooperate with you.

2. Your prompt attention to this matter will be much appreciated.

3. We appreciate your co-operation.

4. We hope this will be a good start for a long and profitable business relationship.

For replying a specific enquiry

1. Thank you very much for your letter of … asking us to quote for …

2. Replying to your enquiry of…, we have the pleasure of quoting of our … as follows.

3. In response to your enquiry of…, we have the pleasure of making you the following offer.

4. We welcome your enquiry dated…quoting…

For closing of a specific enquiry

1. Should your price…we intend to place a large order with you/we may place regular orders for large quantities.

2. If the quality of your … is satisfactory and the prices acceptable/attractive, we shall be able to give you considerable orders/ we could place a firm order.

3. We hope the quotation will prove acceptable to you and are looking forward to receiving your order soon.

4. We hope that our quotation will be acceptable to you, and await your formal orders with keen interest.

Part III
Practical Writing

Main Information

♣ Practice 1

Complete the following chart according to Sample 1.

Source of information: _____

Importer: _____

Intention: _____

Requirements: _____

Key Phrases

Practice 2

Translate the following phrases into Chinese or English.

English	Chinese
in the market for/ be interested in buying sth.	_____
quote sb. a price for sth.	_____
the minimum quantity	_____
date of delivery	_____
provide sb. with sth./provide sth. for sb.	_____
_____	与某人达成交易
_____	大宗订单
_____	按照要求
_____	缺货 / 脱销
_____	不可撤销信用证

Practice 3

Complete the following passage with the proper form of the words or phrases given in the box below.

enquiry	supply	receipt	discount	suit
quote	exceed	specific	appreciate	grant

Dear Sirs,

Thank you for your _____ regarding our iPhone 4S and your desire to enter into a direct business relationship with us.

As requested, we are sending you our _____ sheet covering the types in which you are interested. Unless otherwise stated, all the products can be _____ within five weeks after _____ of your order. For an order _____ 100,000 sets, we usually _____ a 5% quantity _____.

Some of our latest catalogue and sample books have also been sent to you under separate cover for your reference. Should any of the items be _____ for your market, please let us know. As soon as we receive your _____ enquiry, we will make you an offer immediately. Your early reply will be much _____.

Yours faithfully

Useful Expressions

♣ Practice 4

Translate the following sentences into English.

1. 我们对你们在本月《中国对外贸易》（*China Foreign Trade*）上所刊登的广告很感兴趣，现请告知该商品的详细情况。

2. 我们希望你方报被套到广州到岸价的最低价格。

3. 请用 e-mail 向我们报最优价，说明支付条件和装运期。

4. 一旦收到你方具体询盘，我们将立即给你们报最优惠的拉各斯（Lagos）到岸价。

5. 请贵公司对此事认真考虑为感。

6. 贵方自行车报价太高，我方无法接受。

7. 此种包装是这种产品国际市场上的流行包装。

8. 我方的报价是合理的、现实的，符合当前市场的价格水平。

♣ Practice 5

Rewrite the underlined parts in the letter below with two different expressions, but without changing the meaning of the sentences.

Dear Sir,

This company is one of the largest women's handbags importers in San Francisco. ①At present we are in the market for your leather handbags and we sincerely hope to enter into a business relationship with you to promote trade between our two countries.

As we usually place very large orders, we would expect a quantity discount in addition to your list prices, and our terms of payment are normally 30 days bill of exchange, documents against payment. If these conditions interest you, and ②you can meet orders of over 100,000 at one time, ③please send us your lowest quotation CIF San Francisco including our 5% commission.

Other information as to the minimum quantity per color and per design and delivery date would be appreciated. We would be obliged if you would also forward us your current catalogue. We are enclosing an enquiry Sheet No. 3401 and ④your prompt attention to our matter will be much appreciated.

Yours faithfully,

① At present we are in the market for your leather handbags

a. _____

b. _____

② you can meet orders of over 100,000 at one time

a. _____

b. _____

③ please send us your lowest quotation CIF San Francisco including our 5% commission

a. _____

b. _____

④ your prompt attention to our matter will be much appreciated

a. _____

b. _____

Letter Writing

♣ Practice 6

Compose a letter of specific enquiry with the given information.

① together with your best terms CIF Vancouver

② the price is in line with our market

③ We trust you will give us an early reply

④ to be sold in North America countries

⑤ quantity available at present

Dear Sir or Madam,

Subject: bicycles

Our branch in Vancouver has asked us for a quotation for 10,000 sets of bicycles _____. Please let us know what quantities you are able to deliver at regular intervals _____. Meanwhile, please also state as requested in our enquiry sheet your earliest delivery date and _____.

If your quality is good and _____, we are ready to conduct substantial business with you.

_____.

Your faithfully,

Jack Smith

Marketing manager

♣ Practice 7

Write a letter of specific enquiry according to the information given below.

You are a large chain of textile retailers in China and looking for a manufacturer who can supply you with a large variety of curtains for the market. Recently, curtains produced by ABC Company in Canada interest you and you want to purchase. But you need further information such as specifications, quality, terms of payment, discount, earliest date of delivery etc. before you place an order. You also need a full sample of their latest products. Now you write a letter to them with enquiry note No. 121 attached, enquiring specifically for the above.

♣ Practice 8

Complete the reply to the letter of Practice 7 according to the Chinese in the parentheses.

Dear Sirs,

Thank you for your enquiry. ①_____ (很高兴能和贵方建立业务关系). We have enclosed our latest illustrated catalogue and price list. We have curtains in various sizes and different colors. For the material, we make cotton and nylon ones. For all the varieties, we also accept tailor-made orders. Furthermore, we are separately sending you our latest samples as requested and feel confident that you will agree that ②_____ (我方产品质地优良，价格合理).

③_____ (如果订货超过十万件，我们将给予5%的折扣). As to terms of payment, it is our custom to accept payment by irrevocable L/C payable against shipping document. For delivery, we usually arrange all our orders within 30 days after receipt of the covering L/C.

Should you need more information, please let us know. We are looking forward to your first order.

Yours sincerely,

Part IV
Supplementary Reading

Reading One

April 20, 2011

Dear Sir or Madam,

We learnt from Commercial Bank in our city that you are producing hand-made carpets in a large variety of materials and you are one of the leading exporters of carpets in your country. We have a great interest in importing your products.

Please provide us with quotes for the goods listed on the enclosed enquiry Sheet No. 523, giving us your lowest prices CIF Qingdao inclusive of our 3% commission at your earliest convenience. When quoting, please also tell us details of your specifications, minimum quantity per style and state clearly your package, earliest date of delivery, terms of payment and discounts for regular purchases. We shall also appreciate it very much if you will kindly mail us your illustrated catalogue, sample books or even samples if possible.

As this line of goods enjoys an increasing demand at our end, we shall be able to place regular orders for large quantities if your quality is suitable and the price is moderate.

Yours sincerely,

Reading Two

Dear Sir or Madam,

We welcome your enquiry of April 20, with enquiry Note No. 523 and thank you for your interest in our carpets. As requested, we are sending you a copy of the illustrated catalogues with details of our specifications and prices attached. By separate mail, we are also forwarding you today our full range of samples available for export at present.

In order to start a concrete transaction between us, we take the pleasure in making you an offer as follows:

Quantity: 10,000 units per style is our minimum quantity.

Package: Your order is packed in cartons, which are lined with damp-resisting paper, then packed in wooden cases.

Payment: By confirmed, irrevocable L/C payable by draft at sight.

Delivery: to be effected by sea from USA within 60 days to Qingdao after receipt of qualified irrevocable L/C.

Discount: We offer a quantity discount of up to 10%, but we are prepared to give 15% of discount for a quantity over 50,000. For regular order over 20,000 a time, we usually offer 12% of discount.

We are confident that our quotation will be acceptable to you and await your initial order.

Yours sincerely,

Lesson Five ·●●

Firm Offer

Objectives

To be proficient in
◎ understanding the main information and key terms often used in a letter of firm offer
◎ writing a letter of firm offer

Writing Tips

A firm offer has binding force. Once the firm offer is made, the offeror is totally committed and not allowed to change its items within the date of validity.

Here are some guidelines:
● express thanks sincerely;
● state the details of the offer (name, price, specification, shipment, terms of payment, discount, package and date of delivery etc.);
● express the hope for a prompt reply.

Part I
Warm-up Activities

◆ **Discuss in pairs and tell what you will enquire in a firm offer.**

◆ **Discuss in pairs and place the steps reaching a deal of jeans in order.**

① Negotiating for what they disagree

② Sending a quotation of the jeans

③ Asking for detailed information of the jeans

④ Confirming what they have agreed

⑤ Reading an advertisement for jeans

Part II
Sample Study

Sample 1

April 23, 2011

Dear Sir or Madam,

We are very pleased to have your letter of enquiry dated April 14, in which you express your interest in our Type HBS301 Color TV sets and *extend* the wish to *place an order with us.*

In reply, we are making you the following offer: 1,000 sets of Type HBS301 Color TV, at $355 per set CIF Copenhagen including 2% commission, for shipment during June. This offer is *valid, subject* to your reply reaching us by 20 May. Other *terms and conditions* are the same as usual.

As the price of raw material has gone up steadily since this year, we hope you will let us have your *initial* order before further rise in costs.

We are anticipating your early reply.

Yours faithfully,

Sample 2

October 21, 2011

Dear Sir or Madam,

You would like to place an order for Type HBS301 TV sets. We regret it is *a discontinued line,* but we now have a similar product on offer, Type FBS403. It occurs to us that you might be interested in them. A descriptive leaflet is enclosed.

In view of your previous large order, we are giving you the first chance that 20% *discount* will be prepared to be given for offering the complete stock.

We will appreciate a prompt reply because we can put the offer out *in the event of* your not being interested.

Yours sincerely,

Vocabulary

extend	/ɪksˈtend/	v. 延长，延伸；扩大，扩展
valid	/ˈvælɪd/	a. 有效的；合法的
subject	/ˈsʌbdʒɪkt/	a. 服从的；受制于……的
initial	/ɪˈnɪʃəl/	a. 开始的，最初的
discount	/ˈdɪskaʊnt/	n./v. 折扣；贴现；贴现率
place an order with		订购；下单
terms and conditions		条款条件，合同条款
a discontinued line		停止生产的货物
in view of		考虑到；鉴于
in the event of		万一；如果

Notes

1. firm offer 实盘

实盘为受盘人在有效期内表示完全同意，交易立即达成的报盘。

We make you a firm offer subject to reply by 6 p.m. our time, Thursday, 3rd Nov.

兹报实盘，以我方时间 11 月 3 日星期四下午 6 点以前答复为有效。

In making a firm offer, mention should be made of the time of shipment and the mode of payment desired.

在确盘时，必须说明装运期及所要求的付款方式。

send/give/make/ forward an offer	报盘
to accept an offer	接受报盘
to confirm an offer	确认报盘
to decline an offer	拒绝报盘
to entertain an offer	考虑报盘
to extend an offer	延长报盘
to withdraw (cancel) offer	撤回报盘
to renew the offer	恢复报盘

2. subject to 以……为准，以……为条件

Subject to your agreement, we will proceed the contract.

如你方同意，我们就履行合同。

The prices are subject to change.

价格可能有变动。

We are giving you an offer, subject to our prior sale.

现给你方报盘，以先售为准。

subject to the receipt of reply by us before/the arrival of your letter at our end before/receiving your reply before/the reply reaching us before ……前收到你方来信为准

3. It occurs to us that 我们意识到；突然想起

It has occurred to us that Type 21 might suit your article just as well.

我们认为型号 21 的产品也适合你方。

It occurs to us that the contract expires on May 20.

突然想起合同 5 月 20 日终止。

4. in the event of / in the event that 万一；以免；如果

We will put the offer out in the event that you are not interested in our products.

如果你方对我方产品不感兴趣，我方可向其他客户普遍发盘。

In the event of force majeure, neither party shall be responsible for any damage caused by it.

如有不可抗力事件发生，任何一方无须对因其造成的损失承担责任。

 Expressions

For making an offer

1. In reply to your letter of…, we're making an offer as follows.

2. We thank you for your enquiry of…and are pleased to quote as follows…

3. With reference to your enquiry, we make you a firm offer…

4. As requested, we are now making the following offer.

For hope of acceptance

1. We trust you will find our quotation satisfactory and look forward to your reply.

2. As the prices quoted are exceptionally low and likely to rise, we would advise you to place your order without delay.

3. You can take advantage of the strengthening market if you confirm your order immediately.

4. As the market price will rise, it would be to your advantage to place orders without delay.

For valid period

1. This offer is valid, subject to…

2. Our firm offer stands valid before…

3. This offer will remain firm /valid/open/effective until…

4. We will hold our offer open till…

Part III
Practical Writing

Main Information

♣ Practice 1

Complete the following chart according to Sample 1.

Names of items: _____

Price: _____

Shipment date: _____

Intention: _____

Valid period: _____

Key Phrases

♣ Practice 2

Translate the following phrases into Chinese or English.

English	Chinese
make/send/give an offer	_____
put the offer out	_____
in the event of	_____
subject to	_____
without delay	_____
_____	出售
_____	优惠价
_____	保留报盘到……有效
_____	给折扣
_____	鉴于

♣ Practice 3

Complete the following sentences with the proper form of the words or phrases given in the box below.

delay	offer	subject to	take advantage of	occur
anticipate	confirm	accept	out of stock	entertain

1. If you decide to _____ our offer, kindly send us your acceptance.

2. We confirm your enquiry of July 23, asking us to make you a(n) _____ for our products.

3. In reply to your previous letters, we are making you an offer subject to our _____ .

4. We are making you the offer, _____ your acceptance before March 3.

5. We trust the offer will be _____ to you and await your order with keen interest.

6. It has _____ to us that No. 15 might suit your purpose just as well.

7. As the market is declining, we advise you to place an order without _____ .

8. We _____ that you will place a trial order in the near future.

9. If you can provide strong evidence, we can _____ your claim.

10. This kind of mobile phone is _____ now.

Useful Expressions

🍀 Practice 4

Complete the following sentences in English.

1. We confirm 200 吨大米的订单 .

　　　　　　　报下列商品实盘 .

2. We are prepared to 给 3% 的折扣 .

　　　　　　　大量订购 .

3. This offer is valid, subject to 我方最后确认 .

　　　　　　　你方在 5 月 20 日之前接受 .

🍀 Practice 5

Rewrite the underlined parts in the letter below with two different expressions, but without changing the meaning of the sentences.

Dear Sirs,

　　We thank you for your letter of enquiry dated July 12. We are pleased to know that our handicraft bags are in high demand at your market.

　　In reply to your enquiry of July 12,

　　① we would like to make an offer as follows:

　　Handicraft bags: $4.00/PC (CIF New York)

　　Time of shipment: During August-September

　　Package: 20 pieces to a carton

　　Payment: by confirmed irrevocable L/C available by draft at sight to be opened 30 days before the time of shipment.

② <u>We are willing to allow 5% discount for all orders over 1,000 pieces</u>. Under separate cover, we have sent you 2 copies of illustrated catalogue of various brands as per your request.

③ <u>You can rely on us to give your order immediate attention.</u>

Yours faithfully,

① we would like to make an offer as follows

a. _____

b. _____

② We are willing to allow 5% discount for all orders over 1,000 pieces

a. _____

b. _____

③ You can rely on us to give your order immediate attention

a. _____

b. _____

Letter Writing

♣ Practice 6

Compose a letter of firm offer according to the information given below.

① electronic calculators

② as per the buyer's option

③ 3,000 pieces

④ US$ 9.00 per piece CIF New York

⑤ June/July, 2011

⑥ confirmed, irrevocable letter of credit

Dear Sirs,

Thank you for your letter of April 5, asking for a quotation for _____.

Subject to your reply reaching us by May 15, we are pleased to make the following offer:

Package: _____

Quantity: _____

Price: _____

Shipment: _____

Payment: _____ payable by draft at sight to be opened 30 days before the time of shipment.

We look forward to receiving your order and assure you that it will receive our prompt attention.

Yours faithfully,

Practice 7

Write a letter of firm offer according to the information below.

Purpose: reply the letter of July 12

Commodity: refrigerators

Specification: as per attached list

Package: at buyer's option

Quantity: 1,000 sets

Price: US$ 80 net per piece CIF Lagos

Shipment: total quantity to be delivered by 3 equal monthly shipments, August through October 20

Payment: 100% by irrevocable, revolving letter of credit

Enclose: 2 copies of illustrated catalogue of various brands

Practice 8

Complete the letter below according to the Chinese in the parentheses.

Dear Sirs,

    ①_____(我们已收到你方电子邮件询价) for peanuts CFR Rotterdam dated September 25. In reply, we offer firm ②_____ (以你方时间9月30日回复为有效) for 300 metric tons of peanuts at RMB ￥2,000 net per metric ton CFR Rotterdam and any other European Main Ports. Shipment is to be made within two months ③_____ (收到你方订单货款) by L/C payable by sight draft.

    Please note that we have quoted our most favorable price and are unable to entertain any counter offer.

    As you are aware that there has been lately a large demand for the above commodity, ④_____ (这样的需求导致价格的增长). However, you may take advantage of the strengthening market if you will send us an immediate reply.

Yours faithfully,

Part IV
Supplementary Reading

Reading One

Dear Sir or Madam,

    We thank you for your letter of enquiry dated May 8, regarding our different colored sweaters. Subject to your reply reaching us by July 10, we have the pleasure of offering you as follows.

Commodity: Sweaters in different colors

Size: Large (L)　　Medium (M)　　Small (S)

Price: CIF 5% London per dozen in US$

　　　L (210)　　　M (190)　　　S (170)

Shipment: October

Payment: By confirmed irrevocable L/C payable by draft at sight

Package: Sweaters are wrapped in plastic bags and bags packed in standard export cardboard cartons.

Please note that a discount of 5% may be granted for orders of over 1,000 pieces.

If we can be of any further help, please feel free to let us know.

Yours faithfully,

Reading Two

Dear Sir or Madam,

We acknowledge receipt of your letter dated 2nd August, from which we note that you wish to have an offer from us for 240 metric tons of groundnuts.

In reply, we are making you, subject to the receipt of reply by September 20, Beijing time, the following offer:

"240 metric tons of groundnuts, hand-picked, shelled and ungraded at RMB ￥2,700 net per metric ton CFR Hamburg for shipment during October. All Risks and War Risks for 110% of invoice value will be covered."

Please note that we have quoted our most favorable price and unable to entertain any counteroffer.

As you are aware that there has been lately a large demand for the above commodities, such growing demand has doubtlessly resulted in price increase.

We are very grateful if you can send us an immediate reply.

Yours faithfully,

Lesson Six • ● ●

Counter-offer

Objectives

To be proficient in

◎ the main information and key terms often used in a letter of counter-offer

◎ writing a letter of counter-offer

Writing Tips

When making a counter offer, one has to state the terms explicitly and use words very carefully so as to avoid ambiguity or misunderstanding. If the offer is rejected or partially rejected, a letter of rejection or a counter-offer is to be written.

Here are some guidelines:

● express thanks for the offer;

● show regret not to be able to accept;

● state reason for rejecting the offer;

● give advice on how to conclude a business;

● wish future cooperation.

Part I
Warm-up Activities

◆ **Discuss in pairs and write out the four general steps in a business negotiation.**

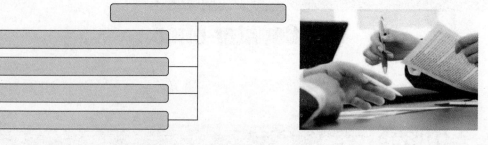

Part II
Sample Study

Sample 1

May 6, 2011

Dear Sir or Madam,

We are *in receipt of* your letter of May 3, offering us cameras at US$400/pc CIF Shanghai.

In reply, we regret to inform you that we find your price *on the high side* and *out of line with* the *prevailing* market level. We do not deny that the quality of your digital cameras is slightly better, but you may be aware that some Japanese dealers are lowering their prices and no doubt there is *keen* competition in the market. Therefore, in any case, the price should be reduced by at least 5%.

We make a counter-offer as follows:

200 cameras at US$380/pc CIF Shanghai, and other terms as per your letter of May 3. As the market is declining, your acceptance is more favorable.

Look forward to your reply.

Yours faithfully,

Sample 2

Dear Sir or Madam,

We thank you for your letter dated May 6, but we regret that we are unable to *entertain* your counter-offer of 200 cameras at US$380/pc CIF Shanghai.

We have to point out that your bid is obviously out of line with the ruling price in the present market, as other buyers in your neighboring countries are buying freely at our quoted price.

Although we are anxious to *conclude the business with* you, we regret that we cannot accept your counter-offer or even *meet you half way*. The best we can do is to reduce our previous quotation by 2%.

We trust that this will meet with your *approval* and look forward to your sales contract. Upon receipt of it, we will open the relative L/C without delay.

Yours faithfully,

Vocabulary

counter-offer	/ˈkaʊntəˈɒfə/	n. 还盘
prevailing	/priˈveɪlɪŋ/	a. 占优势的；主要的
keen	/kiːn/	a. 激烈的，紧张的
entertain	/ˌentəˈteɪn/	v. 招待；款待
approval	/əˈpruːvəl/	n. 批准；认可
in receipt of		收到
on the high side		偏高
out of line with		与……不符
conclude the business with		和……达成交易
meet...half way		折中处理；各让一半

Notes

1. counter-offer

Your counter-offer is not in line with the prevailing market.

你方还盘价格与现行市场不符。

If you cannot accept, please make best possible counter-offer.

如你方不能接受，请尽早还盘。

Our counter-offer is well in line with the international market.

我方还盘完全符合国际市场价格水平。

2. out of line with: not in line with

The price you offered is out of line with the prevailing market, so it is beyond what is acceptable to us.

你方报价与现行市场行情不符，故我方无法接受。

The specifications of the goods are out of line with those stipulated in the contract.

货物的规格与合同所规定的规格不一致。

The US dollar's movement seems to be out of line with the country's macroeconomic conditions.

美元走势似乎与美国宏观经济形势脱轨了。

3. deny   *v.* 否认，拒绝

We do not deny that the quality of groundnut kernels（花生仁）is slightly better.

我们不否认你方花生仁的质量稍微好些。

They denied having received their letter.

他们否认已收到信件。

It cannot be denied that our agents made a mistake.

不否认我方代理搞错了。

4. recommend   *v.* 推荐，劝告

to recommend sb. sth. / recommend sth. to sb.

to recommend + noun

Recommend your immediate acceptance.

劝你方立即接受。

to recommend + gerund

We recommend buying a small quantity for trial.

我们建议你方购买少量试用。

to recommend + that (subjunctive mood)

We recommend that you make a trial of these goods.

建议你方试订这些商品。

to recommend sb. + complement (verb phrase)

We recommend you to place a large order of these goods because they sell well.

我们建议你方大量订购这些商品，因为此类商品正畅销。

5. ruling   *a.* 现行的

ruling price: current/going/present/prevailing/prevalent price 现行价格

The ruling/prevailing price remain strong.

现行价格坚挺。

6. meet sb. half way

In view of our friendly relations, we would meet you half way as a conclusion.

鉴于双方的友好关系，我们各让一半达成交易。

If you really want to settle the problem, we are ready to meet you half way.

如果你们真想解决问题，我们愿意作一半的让步。

If you meet us half way with regard to price, then we can consider placing a bigger order.

如果您愿意在价格上各让一半，我们可以考虑下一张更大的订单。

 Expressions

For receiving an offer

1. We have received your offer of…, offering us…

2. Your letter of…have been duly received, in which you offer us…

3. Thank you for your letter of…, offering us…

4. We are in receipt of your offer of…for…

For expressing regret at being unable to accept the offer

1. We regret to tell you that your price is 10% higher than the average.

2. We regret to inform you that we are unable to accept your prices, which will leave us a very small profit margin.

3. The price you quoted is found to be on the high side.

4. We regret to tell you that our users here find your price too high and out of line with the prevailing market.

For reasons for inability to accept the offer

1. We found that we can obtain from another firm a piece of 5% lower than yours.

2. We are not able to accept your orders because another supplier is offering us the similar quality at a price 3% lower.

3. Information indicates that some Japanese mode parcels have been sold at the level of …

4. We feel that your quotation is not proper because the price of such material is on the decline at present.

For proposal

1. If you can reduce the price by 10%, we can do the business.

2. If you can reduce your price to that extent, we will be pleased to place an order with you.

3. In view of our long friendly relationship, we suggest that you reduce your price by 8%.

4. Should you be prepared to reduce your limit by, say 10%, we might come to terms.

Part III
Practical Writing

Main Information

♣ Practice 1

Complete the following chart according to Sample 1.

Receipt of the offer: _____

Rejection and reasons: _____

Counter proposal: _____

Expectation of the acceptance: _____

Key Phrases

♣ Practice 2

Translate the following phrases into Chinese or English.

English	Chinese
on the high side	_____
reduce the price to	_____
the ruling price	_____
leave… with only a small profit	_____
in receipt of	_____
_____	与……不一致
_____	各让一半
_____	先前报价
_____	做出让步
_____	请注意

♣ Practice 3

Complete the following sentences with the proper form of the words or phrases given in the box.

in a position to	indicate	meet half way	reduce	close business
take the opportunity	minimum	exceed	approve	measure up to

1. We regret to say that the quality does not _____ the contracted standard.

2. If you can make a _____ of 2% in price, we will accept it.

3. We hope that our request will meet with your _____.

4. Owing to _____ demand, we regret that we cannot offer you the type required.

5. Ten tons is the _____ quantity you have to take.

6. We _____ to offer the following new products.

7. If you are prepared to reduce your original price by 3%, we will be able to _____ with you.

8. We can not even _____ you _____ because we make no profit in that case.

9. We do not deny there are _____ that the market is declining.

10. Please let us know when you are _____ supply this commodity.

Useful Expressions

♣ Practice 4

Complete the following sentences in English.

1. Your price is found to be 偏高 .

     与我处的市场行情不符 .

     比日本货高出 30%.

2. We have to point out that 运来的货物品质与合同规定的不符合 .

     你方耽误开证使我方处于困境 .

     我方市场有许多欧洲生产厂家提供的男士衬衫 .

3. Please keep us posted of 你方市场的货物供应情况 .

     你们每月销售电器用品的数量 .

     你们每季度需要进口的数量 .

♣ Practice 5

Rewrite the underlined parts in the letter below with two different expressions, but without changing the meaning of the sentences.

Dear Sir,

  We note from your letter of October 30 that ①you find our price for the subject article is on the high side.

  Much as we would like to cooperate with you in expanding sales, ②we regret that we simply cannot see our way clear to entertain your counter-offer, as the price we quoted is quite realistic. In fact, we have received a lot of orders from various sources at this level.

  ③If you see any chance of change, please let us know. On account of a limited supply available at present, we should ask you to act early.

  In the meantime, ④please keep us posted of development at your end. We assure you that any further enquiries from you will get our prompt attention.

Yours faithfully,

① you find our price for the subject article is on the high side

a. _____

b. _____

② we regret that we simply cannot see our way clear to entertain your counter-offer

a. _____

b. _____

③ If you see any chance of change

a. _____

b. _____

④ please keep us posted of developments at your end

a. _____

b. _____

Letter Writing

🍀 Practice 6

Compose a letter according to the information below.

① Should you be prepared to reduce your limit

② some parcels of Japanese manufacturers have been sold at a level of 10% lower than yours

③ we regret that we find your price too high

④ please email us your reply at your earliest convenience

⑤ offering us 60 tons of subject goods at £135 per ton CFR Shanghai

Dear Sirs,

We thank your for your letter of 10th March _____, on usual terms.

In reply, _____ and out of line with the prevailing market. Information indicates that _____.

As material of similar quality is easily obtained at a much lower price, we find it hard to accept your offer. _____ by 10%, we might come to terms.

It is in view of our long-standing business relationship that we make you such a most favorable counter-offer and _____.

We look forward to hearing from you soon.

Yours truly,

🍀 Practice 7

Write a letter of counter-offer according to the information below.

You have got a letter dated 10th October. The buyer informed that the price for shirts is on the high side, but you think the quoted price is quite realistic. Although you would like to cooperate with your client to expand sales, you cannot see your way clear to entertain the counter-offer. You also tell that you are receiving an offer from another buyer in your area, and the price is 3% higher. Please write a letter to decline the offer.

◆ Practice 8

Complete the letter according to the Chinese in the parentheses.

Dear Sirs,

   We are informed in your letter of March 20 that ①_____ (标题货物的价格持续过高), since Japanese goods are being offered at a price approximately 10% lower than that quoted by us.

   Although we do not doubt about what you say, we think ②_____ (其他厂商的产品质量不如我方). We are desirous to establish our business with you, but we regret that ③_____ (我们不能接受你方还盘甚至折中处理). The best we can do is to make a reduction of 2% in our previous quotation. ④_____ (我们希望你方能着眼于我方产品的高品质).

   We look forward to hearing from you soon.

Yours truly,

Part Ⅳ
Supplementary Reading

Reading One

Dear Sirs,

   RE: COUNTER-OFFER FOR MOTOR BICYCLES

   We thank you for your letter of July 30 offering us 1,000 pieces of captioned motor bicycles.

   We have been very pleased with your products, however, we find that your price is so high that our margin of profit would be very little or nil. Referring to the Sales Confirmation No.564, you can find if we ordered 1,000 motor bicycles with the same brand, the price was 10% lower than your present price. Since we placed the last order in lower price, and the price for raw materials has also been decreased, accepting your present price will mean great loss to us, let alone profit.

We would like to place repeat orders with you if you could reduce your price at least by 2%. It is in view of our long-standing business relationship that we make you such a counter-offer.

We hope you will consider our counter-offer most favorable and give us your reply at your earliest convenience.

Yours faithfully,

Reading Two

Dear Sirs,

Thank you for your letter dated May 15. Much as we would like to do business with you, we regret not being able to accommodate your request to make a better offer than the one we suggested to you.

The price we have quoted is quite reasonable as we always sell those products at US$45/pc, and have received substantial orders at our level. At the same time, we find that you have purchased from us twice as much the first three months of this year as you did in the same period of last year. This indicates to us that you have been successful in retailing our merchandise.

We hope that you will be able to accept our offer. Supplies of this product are limited at this moment, so it is appreciated if you can reply early.

Yours faithfully,

Unit 3

Conclusion of Business

Lesson Seven ●●●

An Order

Objectives

To be proficient in
◎ understanding the main information and key terms often used in an order letter
◎ writing an order letter

Writing Tips

An order letter is a type of business letter which is used to request the supply of a specific quantity of goods. The objective is to provide the seller with detailed instructions for fulfilling the order.

Here are some guidelines:

● tell the seller your intention to place an order directly at the beginning;
● describe in great detail what is being ordered;
● express the willingness to conclude a business at the end of the letter.

Part I
Warm-up Activities

◆ Write out some essential points that an order should contain.

✧ Description of the goods, such as

_____

_____

Quantity

_____

Article number

✧ Package

✧ _____

✧ Time of shipment

◆ **Work in groups and complete the following order letter.**

Dear Mr. Smith,

    Please ship us strawberry jam as per the following terms:

_____	Strawberry Jam, Quality A1
_____	2,6000 Jars
Price	US $3.2 per jar CIF Shenzhen
_____	Seaworthy wooden cases
_____	By October 8, 2011
Mode of transport	Ocean freight

    We are awaiting your acknowledgement.

Yours sincerely,

Part II
Sample Study

Sample 1

December 5, 2011

Dear Sir or Madam,

    Thank you for your quotation of November 25, 2011. We find both quality and prices *satisfactory*. We are pleased to *place a trial order for* the following products:

Quantity	Article No	Prices
120	T256	US $ 25 per unit
120	D278	US $ 30 per unit
		Total US $ 6,600
		CIF Beijing

Payment: by irrevocable L/C, payable by draft at sight

These items are urgently required by our customers. Therefore, we hope that the *consignments* will be *dispatched* before December 23. We trust that you will give special care to the package of the goods, lest the goods should be damaged during transit.

We hope this order is *acceptable* to you and look forward to your prompt response.

Yours faithfully,

Sample 2

Dear Sir or Madam,

Thank you very much for your order of November 5 for Newsmy MP4 player A1 and A28. We are pleased to receive your order and *confirm* as follows:

Quantity	Article No	Prices
120	A1	US $ 25 per unit
120	A28	US $ 30 per unit
		Total US $ 5, 500
		CIF Beijing

Payment: by irrevocable L/C, payable by draft at sight

As the goods you ordered are now in *stock*, we will ship them at the earliest possible convenience.

Your method of payment is acceptable to us. We sincerely hope this order will result in *repeat orders* in the near future.

Yours sincerely,

Vocabulary

order	/'ɔːdə/	*n./v.* 订购；订货；订单
satisfactory	/ˌsætɪs'fæktərɪ/	*a.* 良好的；令人满意的
consignment	/kən'saɪnmənt/	*n.* 交付，委托；托运
dispatch	/dɪ'spætʃ/	*v.* 派遣（某人）；发送（某物）
acceptable	/ək'septəbl/	*a.* 可接受的；容许的
confirm	/kən'fɜːm/	*v.* 证实；肯定，确定
stock	/stɒk/	*n.* 存货，库存
place a trial order for		试订
repeat orders		续订

Notes

1. satisfactory

satisfied   感到满意的

We find both the quality and price satisfactory.

认为质量和价格都令人满意。

As we have complete confidence in you, we shall rely on you to execute the contract satisfactorily.

我们对贵方完全信任，所以我们相信贵方会令人满意地履行合同。

We are satisfied with the smoothness of the negotiation.

我们对谈判的顺利进行很满意。

2. confirm

to confirm an order   确认订单

confirmation   n. 证实；确定

Please fax us your confirmation as soon as possible.

请尽快用传真告知你方的确认。

We confirm that deliveries will be made on schedule.

兹确认按照计划完成交货。

3. consignment

consignment goods   寄售货物

consignment note   发货通知书

consignment records   寄售记录

We will ship all the two hundred sets in one consignment.

我们将全部200台一批发送。

We usually only order goods on consignment.

我们通常只能订购寄售的货物。

The consignment covering our Order No 123 arrived last week.

我方第123号订单项下货物已于上周运到。

consign   v. 托运，委托

consign the goods   寄售货物

consignor = shipper   发货人

consignee   收货人

The goods will be consigned in three lots.

货物将分三批发运。

4. stock

You can supply us from stock.

你们可供现货。

Our stocks are rapidly running short (low).

我们的存货越来越少。

in stock (out of stock) 有（无）存货

We confirm that the required items are in stock.

贵方所需的各项产品，均以现货供应，特此奉告。

As the goods you ordered are now in stock, we will ship them without delay. 因为贵方订货尚有存货，本公司将一定尽快装运。

We regret to inform you that the goods you ordered are out of stock at present.

我们遗憾地告知贵方，你方所订货物目前缺货。

5. repeat order

firm order	正式订单	additional order	追加订货（单）
sample order/order by sample	凭样订单	fresh/new order	新订（单）
initial order	初次订单/初次订货	trial order	试订（单）
duplicate order	重复订单/再订货		

相关动词词组

to take an order/ to book an order	下订单
to accept an order/ to take an order	接受订单
to close an order	决定成交
to cancel an order	取消订单
to confirm an order	确认订单
to fill/execute an order	执行订单

6. dispatch

dispatch the goods　　　　　　发运货物

We hope you can dispatch the goods within the stipulated time.

希望你方能在规定期限内发货。

Because the quality of the goods dispatched by you is not in accordance with the contract, we have the right to refuse the goods.

因你方所交货物质量与合同不符，我们有权拒收。

We'll do our utmost to ensure the prompt dispatch of the goods to your port.

我们会尽一切可能确保货物准时发运至你方港口。

For such a big order, we propose to have the goods dispatched via sea.

数量如此多的货物，我们建议走海运。

 Expressions

For intention

1. We have the pleasure of sending you an order for…

2. Your terms and conditions are satisfactory and we would like to place an order with you for…

3. We have received your catalogue and price list, and now we want to order the following

goods at the named prices.

4. We have received your quotation of … and enclose our official order form.

For acceptance

1. We wish to refer to the recent exchange of emails and are pleased to confirm with you a transaction of…

2. We thank you for your order number … and will dispatch the goods by…

3. We have sent our confirmation of your order and you are requested to open the L/C as soon as possible.

4. We were pleased to receive your order of…for…, and welcome you as one of our customers.

For refusal

1. To our regret, we are unable to accept your order for…, since…

2. We regret that we are not in a position to entertain any further orders.

3. We are sorry to inform you that the goods ordered on … cannot be supplied.

4. As…, we regret our inability to entertain any new orders.

Part III Practical Writing

Main Information

◆ Practice 1

Complete the following chart according to Sample 1.

Port of destination: _____

Term of payment: _____

Intention: _____

Requirements: _____

Key Phrases

◆ Practice 2

Translate the following phrases into Chinese or English.

English	Chinese
_____	与……一致
_____	订单
_____	处理订单，备货
_____	缺货
_____	寄售货物
find both quality and price satisfactory	_____

give special care to

be unable (not in a position) to accept one's order

confirm with sb. the order of…

repeat order

_____

_____

_____

_____

♣ Practice 3

Complete the following sentences with the proper form of the words given in the box below.

order	urgency	dispatch	regular	execute
confirmation	cancel	quotation	agreeable	stock

1. We regret that we have to _____ our order because of the inferior quality of your products.

2. Your prompt _____ of our order will be appreciated.

3. We are in _____ need of the goods, so we hope you will effect prompt delivery.

4. We are _____ to your proposal for payment terms.

5. Thank you for your Order No. 67. We accept it and will _____ the goods next week.

6. The goods you ordered are momentarily out of _____ .

7. We are arranging for the shipment of the _____ goods.

8. We thank you for your _____ of Oct. 15 and are placing an order with you for the following items.

9. We _____ with you the following order for a man's leather jacket at the price stated in your letter.

10. If the quality of your product is satisfactory, we expect to place _____ orders for significant quantities.

Useful Expressions

♣ Practice 4

Rewrite the underlined parts in the letter below with two different expressions, but without changing the meaning of the sentences.

Dear Sir,

Thank you for your quotation and samples of August 11.

We find both the price and quality of your products satisfactory and ①we take pleasure in placing an order for 3,000 pairs PU artificial leather slippers. ②Enclosed please find No. 321.

As the goods are urgently required by our customers, ③we expect the delivery to occur before August 22.

We will submit further orders if this one is completed to our satisfactory.

Yours sincerely,

①we take pleasure in placing an order with you for

a. _____

b. _____

②Enclosed please find No.321

a. _____

b. _____

③we expect the delivery to occur before August 22

a. _____

b. _____

♣ Practice 5

Complete the following sentences in English.

1. We are glad that _____ (经过双方长期友好的协商，现已达成交易).

2. _____ (由于双方的共同努力，我们达成了交易) and hope it is a good beginning.

3. We believe you will do your utmost to _____ (执行我方第一笔订单) as it will lead to a series of transactions between us.

4. _____ (兹随函附上试订单一份). If the quality is up to our expectation, we shall send further orders in the near future.

5. We have sent our confirmation of your order and _____ (望尽快开立信用证).

6. _____ (我们尚有一些库存), and should be able to meet your requirements if you wish to duplicate your last order.

7. _____ (我方第 76 号订单项下货物) will be arrived next Friday.

8. We hope you will find the goods satisfactory and we _____ (期待还能收到贵方的订单).

Letter Writing

♣ Practice 6

Compose a letter of order with the given information.

① you will give special care to the package of the goods

② within a week after receipt of the relative L/C

③ We are pleased to confirm having purchased from you

④ under the following terms and conditions

⑤ We are now arranging the establishment of the L/C

Aug. 24, 2011

Yongxin Electronics Import & Export Corporation

167 Tongtai Avenue, Baiyun District, Guangzhou

Guangdong, China

Dear Sirs,

Subject: Confirmation of the order for 1,500 sets of Changhong Color TV (42 inches)

_____ 1,500 sets of Changhong Color TV (42 inches) _____:

1,500 sets of Changhong Color TV (42 inches), at US$350 CIF Thailand, packed in wooden cases, each containing 6 sets, shipment from Shanghai to Bangkok _____.

We trust that _____, lest the goods should be damaged in transit.

_____, which will be opened in your favor upon receipt of your sales confirmation.

Yours faithfully,

Harlin Ward

Harlin Ward

Sales Manager

♣ Practice 7

Complete a letter of order according to the Chinese in the parentheses.

November 28, 2011

Dear Eunice,

Thank you for your quotation of November 20. ①_____ (我们接受贵方的价格，并确认我们的正式订单HK-010）as per the copy enclosed. The formal order sheet will be followed by post.

Please do 100% testing before shipment to ensure the quality and ②_____ (按说明及时装运货物).

Please confirm your acceptance by e-mail and send us your Proforma Invoice for opening L/C. ③_____ (我方将继续订货) if this one is completed satisfactorily.

Your early reply will be highly appreciated.

Yours sincerely,

Penny Turner

♣ Practice 8

Complete the reply to the letter of Practice 7 according to the information given below.

感谢 11 月 28 日的来信，确认已收到 HK-010 订单，同时也承诺于出货前将遵照订单上规定做 100% 测试。附上已签订单，及供开 L/C 用的 P/I。希望首次订单的处理将促成双方进一步合作，并开始友好业务往来。

Part IV Supplementary Reading

Reading One

Dear Sirs,

Sub: Order for 2,000 Pairs of Sheep Leather Gloves

Please dispatch to us 2,000 pairs of sheep leather gloves as per the terms stated in your offer of May 5.

We want you to take special care of the quality and the packing of this order. The leather should be of the same quality as that used in the samples. We hope that you can package each pair in an airtight polythene bag, a dozen pairs of gloves in a box and then 20 boxes to a strong seaworthy wooden case.

Please confirm that you can execute our order before the end of May, as the opening of the store is planned for the beginning of August. We will submit further orders if this one is satisfactorily completed.

We hope this order is acceptable to you and look forward to your early reply.

Yours Sincerely,

Reading Two

Dear Sirs,

We thank you very much for your kind order for our tea which we have received. It has our immediate and careful attention.

You may rest assured that the tea in the order has been carefully packaged in the chest to prevent damage in transit. We shall send you the shipping advice and the invoice at the time of shipment by this May.

The terms of payment you have suggested are acceptable, and you can rely on us to give all your orders prompt attention.

Since it is the best season for tea, we hope you make full use of the opportunity. I am sure you will be pleased to receive good comments about our tea from your consumers, and build up a market for the product in your country.

We hope this will lead to more substantial orders.

Yours sincerely,

Lesson Eight ·••

Sending Contract

Objectives

To be proficient in
◎ understanding the definition and content of a contract
◎ writing a letter of sending a contract

Writing Tips

When a seller or a buyer completely agrees with the terms and conditions of an offer, order or a counter-offer in the business, he will send a sales contract/confirmation or a purchase contract/confirmation to the other side to ask for counter-signature.

In sending out the above contracts or confirmations, special attention should be paid to the price, payment terms, specifications, quality, quantity, time of delivery, port of destination, etc.

Here are some guidelines:
● the letter should not be too long but be clear and accurate;
● the information you offer in the letter should be as authentic and credible as possible because any error may cause unexpected trouble;
● the format and layout should be standardized and printed neatly.

Part I
Warm-up Activities

◆ Read the following sales contract and fill in the blanks with the items given below.

Unit Price	Terms of Payment	Quantity	Time of Shipment
Specification	Port of Destination	Packing	Commodity

- Contract NO.0512
- SELLERS: Shenxing Printing & Dying Co., Ltd.
- BUYERS: Sono Handels AG
- _____   _____   _____   _____

Bedding Set	8021	2,000	$18
Bedding Set	8011	1,000	$15
Baby Set	8036	1,000	$9

- (All the prices are CFR Basel)
- _____: Be packed individually in plastic bags at one dozen to a carton
- Shipping Mark: At seller's option
- Insurance: To be covered by the buyer
- _____: arriving at the port of Basel not later than the 28th May, 2011
- Port of Shipment: Shanghai
- _____: Basel
- _____: D/P 30 days

◆ Work in pairs and write out some other items included in a contract besides what mentioned above.

_____

_____

Arbitration Clause

Part II
Sample Study

Sample 1

Dear Sir or Madam,

    We refer to the recent exchange of emails and are pleased to confirm having concluded with you a transaction of 4,000 dozen men's shirts.

    Enclosed you will find our *Sales Contract* No.354 in *duplicate*. Please *countersign* and return one copy to us for our file. We trust you will open the relative L/C at an early date. The *stipulations* in the relative credit should strictly *conform* to the terms stated in our Sales Contract.

    As regards additional quantities, we are working on this and will let you have an offer sometime next week.

Yours faithfully,

Sample 2

Dear Sir or Madam,

    We have *duly* received your S/C No.354 covering 4,000 dozen men's shirts we have booked with you. Enclosed please find the duplicate with our counter-signature. Thanks to our mutual efforts, we were able to bridge the price gap and put the deal through.

    The relative L/C has been established *in your favor* on May 21 to the Bank of China in Beijing. It will reach you *in due course*.

    We trust this order will be the first of a series of deals between us.

Yours faithfully,

Vocabulary

duplicate	/'duːpləkeɪt/	*n.* 副本，抄件
countersign	/'kaʊntəsaɪn/	*v.* 副署，会签
stipulation	/ˌstɪpjʊ'leɪʃən/	*n.* 条款，约定，（规定的）条件
conform	/kən'fɔːm/	*v.* 使一致，遵从
duly	/'duːlɪ/	*ad.* 按时地，及时地

in your favor　　　　　　　　　　以你方为抬头

in due course　　　　　　　　　　及时地，在适当的时候

Sales Contract　　　　　　　　　销售合同，售货合同

 Notes

1. contract　　　　　　　　　*n.* 合同，合约，契约

originals of the contract　　合同正本

copies of the contract　　　合同副本

purchase contract　　　　　购货合同，订购合同

make/place/sign a contract　签订合同

draw up a contract　　　　　拟订合同

draft a contract　　　　　　起草合同

land a contract　　　　　　得到合同

contractual　　　　　　　　*a.* 合同的，契约的

contractual condition　　　合同交易条件

contractual damage　　　　合同引起的损害

contractor　　　　　　　　*n.* 订约人，承包人

We can repeat the contract on the same terms.

我们可以按照同样的条款再订一个合同。

As per the contract, the construction of the factory is now under way.

根据合同规定，工厂的建设正在进行中。

Who are the contractors of the two respective parties?

协议双方的订约人分别是谁？

2. for one's file (for one's records)　供某人存档；供……存查

complete one's records　　　　　供某人存档、归档

be on file　　　　　　　　　　　存档；归档

Here is our file on the Asia Market.

这是我方关于亚洲市场的存档资料。

3. stipulation

on the stipulation that...　　　以……为条件，在……条件下

Please see that the L/C stipulation will strictly conform with the contract terms.

请注意做到信用证规定与合同条款须严格一致。

stipulate　　*v.* 规定，保证

Our contract stipulates that insurance should be effected for 110% only.

我们的合同规定仅以 110% 投保。

We have no objection to the stipulations about the packing and shipping mark.

我们同意关于包装和运输唛头的条款。

The contract stipulates that the goods (should) be shipped entirely.

合同规定货物全部转运。

4. duplicate　　　　　*v.* 重复，使再发生

We have some stock left, and shall be able to meet your requirements if you wish to
duplicate your last order.

如果你愿意接上次订单续订，我们有一些库存能满足你的要求。

duplicate　　　　　　*n.* 副本

Please send back the countersigned duplicate duly.

会签后请寄回副本。

duplicate　　　　　　*a.* 完全相同的

As the market has now advanced, we cannot execute a duplicate order.

随着市场的增长，我们无法再执行同样的订单。

in duplicate/in two copies/ in two originals　　　　　　一式两份

in triplicate　　一式三份　　in quadruplicate　　　　一式四份

5. countersign

We attach hereto our Purchase Contract No. 356 with our signature. Please check and countersign it.

现附上我们已经签署的 356 号购货合同，请审核并会签。

counter-signature

We enclose our S/C No. 476 in duplicate for your counter-signature.

现附上我方 476 号售货合同一式两份，请会签。

6. conform

conform to　　　　　遵从；符合

conform with　　　　符合；遵守

conformity　　　　　*n.* 符合；一致

be in conformity with /be in line with/be in accordance with

与……相一致；依照

The quality must conform to the sample.

质量必须与货样相符。

Your proposal does not conform with our arrangements.

你方的建议与我们商定的办法不一致。

7. as requested/on request

As requested, we will inform you of the dispatch date immediately upon completion of
shipment.

按照你方要求，我们会在装运完成后立即将发货日期通知你方。

We hope you can give prompt attention to our request for the establishment of business relations.

我们希望你们能及时处理我们建立业务关系的要求。

As requested, we now hold this offer open for a further 5 days since 24th April.

按你方要求，我方报价有效期从 4 月 24 日起延长 5 日。

Content of a Sales Contract

◇ Title —— 合同名称及其编号。

◇ Preamble —— 序文：包括签约日期、地点、当事人名称、地址及其法律地位。

◇ Name of Commodity —— 商品名称。

◇ Quality Clause —— 品质条款：包括约定品质的决定方式及其时间和地点。

◇ Quantity Clause —— 数量条款：包括约定数量单位、交付数量的决定时间和地点，以及溢短装数量的解决办法等。

◇ Price Clause —— 价格条款：包括价格种类、结构、使用货币计算单位以及币值或价格变动风险的归宿等。

◇ Packing Clause —— 包装条款：包括包装的方式、方法、包装的材料以及唛头等。

◇ Delivery Clause —— 交货期：包括交货时间、地点、交货方式、交货通知等。

◇ Payment Clause —— 支付条款：包括支付方式、支付工具以及支付时间等。

◇ Insurance Clause —— 保险条款：包括由何方保险、投保险别、金额与货币、约定保险人等。

◇ Inspection Clause —— 检验条款：包括项目、检验时间与地点、检验机构、检验方法、检验效力及其费用的负担等。

◇ Claim Clause —— 索赔条款：包括索赔的期限及其通知方法、应提出的证明文件、索赔货物和付款的关系，以及解决索赔的基本原则。

◇ Arbitration Clause —— 仲裁条款：包括范围、地点、仲裁机构及其费用的负担等。

 Expressions

For description of contract enclosed

1. We are pleased to enclose two copies of our contract...

2. We are enclosing our S/C … in duplicate.

3. Our P/C… in two originals was airmailed to you.

For intention of getting countersignature

1. You will receive our S/C No…and please countersign and return one copy to us for file.

2. We are now sending you our S/C No...please sign and send it back for our file.

3. This is our S/C No… If you find the content there agreeable, please countersign and return one copy for our records.

Part III Practical Writing

Main Information

Practice 1

Complete the following chart according to Sample 1.

Name of commodity: _____

Quantity: _____

Intention: _____

Requirements: _____

Key Phrases

Practice 2

Translate the following phrases into Chinese or English.

English	Chinese
in duplicate	_____
name of commodity and specifications	_____
for opening the L/C	_____
for your record	_____
issuing bank / opening bank	_____
_____	购货合同
_____	一般条款
_____	与……严格相符
_____	副署，会签
_____	如所要求

Practice 3

Complete the following sentences with the proper form of the words or phrases given in the box below.

mutual	conform	stipulation	request
countersign	file	duplicate	in due course

1. We acknowledge with thanks the receipt of your order dated 5th May, which we assure you, shall be executed _____ .

2. I believe the contract will redound to our _____ benefit.

3. Please be assured that we shall carry out your order in strict accordance with the contract _____ .

4. When the sales contract has been signed by the seller, it will be _____ by the buyer.

5. We have duly countersigned the contract and returned one copy for your _____ .

6. There are the original contracts in _____ we have prepared.

7. Your proposal does not _____ with our arrangements.

8. We are sending herewith our Sales Confirmation No.23 in triplicate at your _____ .

Useful Expressions

Practice 4

Translate the following sentences into English.
1. 请注意信用证的条款应与我方销售合同的条款严格一致。
2. 我们已经收到你方第 115 号销售合同一式两份。
3. 我保证我们能按合同规定如期装船。
4. 如果没有异议，请签字并返还销售合同副本以供我方存档。
5. 现附上我们已会签的第 546 号采购合同。
6. 按合同规定，货物在下月底前运出。

Practice 5

Rewrite the underlined parts in the letter below with two different expressions, but without changing the meaning of the sentences.

> Dear Sir,
>
>   With reference to our recent exchange of emails, ①we are pleased to confirm the transaction for 600 bales of Grade I crumb rubber.
>
>   ②We enclosed our Sales Contract No.759 in duplicate. ③Please countersign and return the bottom copy to us for our records. We will be grateful if you can open the necessary letter of credit as soon as possible.
>
>   With regard to additional quantities, we are studying the supply situation and will let you have an offer about a week's time.
>
> Yours sincerely,

① we are pleased to confirm our having concluded the transaction

a. _____

b. _____

② We enclosed our Sales Contract No. 759 in duplicate

a. _____

b. _____

③ Please countersign and return the bottom copy to us for our records

a. _____

b. _____

Letter Writing

❧ Practice 6

Compose a letter of sending S/C with the given information.

① Enclosed are two copies of our Sales Contract No. 224

② shall deliver them to you as the time stipulated

③ look forward to your further orders

④ We are very glad to come to a final agreement

⑤ enable us to effect shipment before the deadline

⑥ Please sign and return one copy for our file

January 15, 2011

Australia Trading Co. Ltd

CO.89-91 Barnett Ave Glynde SA, Australia

Dear Sirs,

    Thank you for order No. ST678. _____ and can finalize this deal with you.

    _____ made out against the said order. _____.

    We understand your urgent need of the goods and _____. Please issue the relevant

L/C so as to _____.

    We appreciate your cooperation and _____.

Yours faithfully,

Dongguan Happy Children Toys Imp/Exp Corp

Qingdong Wang

Qingdong Wang

Sales Manager

❧ Practice 7

Complete the following letter according to the Chinese in the parentheses.

Dear Sirs,

    Many thanks for your order BK357 for 3,500 sets of cups and saucers.

    We are very glad to confirm acceptance of your order and ①_____ (将在本月底安排装运). We have no doubt that the goods will reach you in time and will give you much satisfaction.

    ②_____ (随函附上我方第987号销售合同一式两份). Please countersign and ③_____ (退回一份供我们存档). In order to effect shipment as required, ④_____ (请在5月底前尽快开立相关信用证).

    We trust that this business may prove to our mutual advantage and appreciate your prompt reply.

Yours truly,

♣ Practice 8

Write the reply to the letter of Practice 7 according to the information below.

- You have received S/C No. 987 in duplicate
- You countersigned and returned one copy
- Express thanks for their cooperation
- You have opened an L/C
- You are prepared to order another 1,000 sets

Part Ⅳ Supplementary Reading

Reading One

Dear Sirs,

Thank you for your order of June 12 for 2,000 sets of bed-sheets and pillowcases. We are very glad to confirm acceptance of your order and will arrange shipment by the end of next month. We trust that the goods will arrive in due time and fully meet your requirements.

We enclose our Sales Contract No.850 in duplicate. Please sign the bottom copy and return it to us for our files as soon as possible. It is stipulated in our S/C that the L/C should be opened in our favor 30 days before making shipment. Please note that the stipulations in the relevant credit should fully conform with the terms as stated in our S/C in order to avoid subsequent amendments.

I am convinced that, with joint effort, business between us will develop to our mutual benefit.

Yours faithfully,

Reading Two

UNIVERSAL TRADING CO., LTD,

Rm 1201-1216 Mayling Plaza, 131 Dongfang, Shanghai, China Zip: 2001120

Tel: 021-58818844 58818766 Fax: 021-58818840

售货合同

SALES CONTRACT

合同日期
DATE: MARCH 27 1998

1. 卖方：环宇贸易有限公司

THE SELLERS: UNIVERSAL TRADING CO., LTD.

合同编号

S/C NO.HY98CS004

2. 地址：中国上海浦东东方路 131 号美陵广场 1201-1216 室

ADDRESS: RM 1201-1216 MAYLING PLAZA, 131 DONGFANG ROAD, SHANGHAI, CHINA.

TEL: 021-58818844; 58818766 FAX: 021-58818840

E-MAIL: youngl@www.universal.com.cn

3. 买方：

THE BUYERS: TIVOL PRODUCTS PLC

4. 地址：

ADDRESS: BERSTOFSGADE 48, ROTTERDAM, THE NETHERLANDS

TEL: +(31) 74 12 37 21 FAX: +(31) 74 12 37 37

E-MAIL: chila@www.tvl.com.ntl

买卖双方同意按下列条件购进、售出下列商品：

THE SELLERS AGREE TO SELL AND THE BUYERS AGREE TO BUY THE UNDER-MENTIONED GOODS ACCORDING TO THE TERMS AND CONDITIONS AS STIPULATED BELOW

商品名称及规格 NAME OF COMMODITY & SPECIFICATION	数量 QUANTITY	单价 UNIT PRICE	总值 TOTAL VALUE
PLUSH TOYS			CIF3% AMSTERDAM
Art.No.KB0677 New Design Brown Bear	1080sets	USD$13.35	USD$14,418.00
Art.No.KB7900 Toy Bear in Sweater	1208pcs	USD$9.30	USD$11,234.40
Art.No.KB2273 Charming Pig	4140pcs	USD$4.70	USD$19,458.00
Art.No.KC2048 Long Hair Cat	3150pcs	USD$6.65	USD$20,947.50
Art.No.KB0278 Plush Twin Bear	1880sets	USD$13.30	USD$25,004.00
			USD$91,061.90

5. 包装：

PACKING: PACKED IN CARTONS OF 8 SETS (KB0677), 8 PCS. (KB7900), 60 PCS. (KP2273), 30 PCS. (KC2048) AND 4 SETS (KB0278) EACH ONLY.

6. 唛头：

SHIPPING MARKS: WILL BE INDICATED IN THE LETTER OF CREDIT.

7. 装船港口：

PORT OF SHIPMENT: SHANGHAI, CHINA

8. 目的港口：

PORT OF DESTINATION: AMSTERDAM THE NETHERLANDS

9. 装船期限：

TIME OF SHIPMENT: NOT LATER THAN MAY 31ST, 1998.

10. 付款条件：

买方应通过买卖双方都接受的银行向卖方开出以卖方为受益人的不可撤销、可转让的即期付款信用证并允许分装、转船。信用证必须在装船前 30 天开到卖方，信用证有效期限延至装运日期后 21 天在中国到期。

TERMS OF PAYMENT: The Buyers shall open with a bank to be accepted by both the Buyers and Sellers an irrevocable transferable letter of credit, allowing partial shipment, transshipment in favor of the Seller and addressed to Sellers payable at sight against first presentation of the shipping document to Opening Bank. The covering letter of credit must reach the Sellers 30 days before shipment, and is valid in China until the 21st day after shipment.

11. 保险：由买方 / 卖方按发票金额加成 10% 投保一切险及战争险。如果买方要求加投上述保险或保险金额超出上述金额，必须提前征得卖方的同意；超出保险费由买方承担。

INSURANCE: To be covered by the Buyers/Sellers for the full invoice valve plus 10% against all risks and war risks. If the Buyers desire to cover for any other extra risks besides aforementioned or amount exceeding the aforementioned limited, the Sellers' approval must be obtained beforehand and all the additional premiums thus incurred shall be for the Buyers' account.

12. 检验：由中国商检局出具的品质 / 重量证明书将作为装运品质数量证明。

INSPECTION: The inspection Certificate of Quality/Weight issued by CCIB shall be taken as basis for the shipping quality/weight.

13. 不可抗力：因人力不可抗拒事故，使卖方不能在合同规定期限内交货或不能交货，卖方不负责任，但是卖方必须立即以电报通知买方。如果买方提出要求，卖方应以挂号函向买方提供由中国国际贸易促进会或有关机构出具的证明，证明事故的存在。

FORCE MAJEURE: The Sellers shall not be held responsible if they, owing to Force Majeure causes, fail to make delivery within the time stipulated in the contract or can't deliver the goods. However, in such a case the sellers shall inform the Buyers immediately by cable. The Sellers shall send to the Buyers by registered letter at the quest of the Buyers a certificate attesting the existence of such a cause or causes issued by China Council for the Promotion of International Trade or by a competent Authority.

14. 异议索赔：品质异议须于货到目的口岸之日起 30 天内提出，数量异议须于货到目的口岸之日起 15 天内提出，买方需同时提供双方同意的公证行的检验证明。卖方将根据具体情况解决异议。由自然原因或船方、保险商责任造成的损失，将不予考虑任何索赔，信用证未在合同指定日期内到达卖方，或 FOB 条款下、买方未按时派船到指定港口，或信用证与合同条款不符，买方未在接到卖方通知所规定的期限内电改有关条款时，卖方有权撤消合同或延迟交货，并有权提出索赔。

DISCREPANCY AND CLAIM: In case discrepancy on quality of the goods is found by the Buyers after arrival of the goods at port of destination, claim may be lodged within 30 days after arrival of the goods at port of destination, while for quantity discrepancy, claim may be lodged within 15 days after arrival of the goods at port of destination, being supported by Inspection Certificate issued by a reputable public surveyor agreed upon by both party. The Seller shall, then consider the claim in the light of actual circumstance. For the losses due to natural cause or causes falling within the responsibilities of the Ship-owners or the Underwriters, the Sellers shall not consider any claim for compensation. In case the Letter of Credit not reach the Sellers within the time stipulated in the Contract, or under FOB price terms Buyers do not send vessel to appointed ports or the Letter of Credit opened by the Buyers does not correspond to the Contract terms and the Buyers fail to amend therefore its terms by telegraph within the time limit after receipt of notification by the Sellers, the Sellers shall have right to cancel the contract or to delay the delivery of the goods and shall have also the right to lodge claims for compensation of losses.

15. 仲裁：凡因执行本合同所发生的或与合同有关的一切争议，双方应友好协商解决。如果协商不能解决应提交中国国际经济贸易仲裁委员会。根据该委员会的有关仲裁程序暂行规则在中国进行仲裁的、仲裁裁决是终局的，对双方都有约束力。仲裁费用除另有裁决外由败诉一方承担。

ARBITRATION: All disputes in connection with the contract or the execution thereof, shall be settled amicably by negotiation. In case no settlement can be reached, the case under dispute may then be submitted to the "China International Economic and Trade Arbitration Commission" for arbitration. The arbitration shall take place in China and shall be executed in accordance with the provisional rules of Procedure of the said Commission and the decision made by the Commission shall be accepted as final binding upon both parties for settling the dispute. The fees, for arbitration shall be borne by the losing party unless otherwise awarded.

卖方：	买方：
THE SELLERS:	THE BUYERS:
UNIVERSAL TRADING CO., LTD.	TIVOL PRODUCTS PLC
SHANGHAI CHINA	ROTTERDAM THE NETHERLAND

Unit 4

Terms of Payment

Lesson Nine ●●●

Negotiating Payment Terms

Objectives

To be proficient in

◎ understanding the main information and key terms often used in a letter negotiating payment terms

◎ writing a letter negotiating payment terms

Writing Tips

Payment is important in the course of business. Payment in international trade is more sophisticated than that in domestic trade. The commonly used methods of payment in international trade are advance payment, L/C (letter of credit), D/P (documents against payment), D/A (documents against acceptance) and O/A (open account). From the perspective of the seller, L/C is better than D/P, D/P at sight is better than D/P after sight, whereas D/P is better than D/A.

Here are some guidelines:

● Favorable payment terms should be stated precisely and politely.

● The reasons for favorable payment terms should be stated clearly.

Part ①
Warm-up Activities

◆ **Write out the full names of the banks whose logos are shown below.**

◆ **Please choose the services banks provide in relation to payment in international trade.**

① Credit Card

④ Letter of Credit

② Collection

⑤ Advance Payment

③ Open Account

⑥ Remittance

Part II
Sample Study

Sample 1

September 11, 2011

Dear Sirs,

Thank you for your letter of August 26. We are glad that we have successfully finalized a transaction in the amount of 8,000 dollars. But, much to our regret, you have still asked for payment by confirmed, *irrevocable* L/C.

Payment by L/C is rather *inconvenient* to a customer like us who has only *moderate* cash reserves on hand. From the moment to open an L/C, and to the time when our buyers pay us, our funds will be tied up for three months. This may cause delay in the execution of this contract.

Moreover, it is not economical to have an L/C opened because the charges involved are too big for such a small volume of business. This being the case, we shall be grateful if you would extend an accommodation to us and comply with our request for D/A terms.

We wish to receive your reply at an early date.

Yours sincerely,

Sample 2

October 6, 2011

Dear Sir or Madam,

We are in receipt of your letter dated September 11 and are pleased to learn of your intention to *promote* our toys in your market.

We have carefully considered your request for payment by D/A terms. But we regret to inform you that we are unable to accept D/A payment terms which will also tie up our funds.

As a rule, we usually do business with clients *on the basis of* sight L/C, as L/C gives us the additional protection of banker's *guarantee*. However, in view of our long friendly business relationship and the small amount involved in this transaction, we are prepared to *grant* you easier payment terms. D/P payment term is acceptable to us.

We look forward to your early and *affirmative* reply.

Yours sincerely,

Vocabulary

irrevocable	/ɪ'revəkəbəl/	a. 不可改变的，不可撤销的
inconvenient	/ˌɪnkən'vɪnjənt/	a. 引起麻烦的，不方便的
moderate	/'mɒdərɪt/	a. 适度的，中等的
promote	/prə'məʊt/	v. 推销；促进
guarantee	/ˌgærən'tiː/	n. 保证；担保，担保人
grant	/graːnt/	v. (正式)给予，允许（所求）
affirmative	/ə'fɜːmətɪv/	a. 肯定的，同意的
on the basis of		以……为基础，在……基础上

Notes

1. irrevocable L/C 不可撤销信用证

It is stipulated in the contract that payment should be made by irrevocable L/C payable by sight draft.

合同规定以不可撤销即期信用证汇票付款。

As agreed upon in our negotiations, payment is to be made by irrevocable L/C.

根据双方谈判所达成的一致，我们将用不可撤销的信用证支付。

If the amount exceeds that figure, payment by confirmed, irrevocable L/C will be requested.

如果货款超过那个数额，我们要求用保兑的、不可撤销的信用证支付。

国际贸易中常见的信用证类型

Documentary L/C	跟单信用证
Confirmed L/C	保兑信用证
Transferable L/C	可转让信用证
Revolving L/C	循环信用证
Sight L/C	即期信用证
Time/ Usance / Term L/C	远期信用证

2. inconvenient

It will be inconvenient for us to arrange shipment at such short notice.

在如此短的时间内安排装运会给我方带来不便。

inconvenience *n.* 不便，麻烦，困难

We apologize for the delay of shipment and regret any inconvenience arising from this.

我们对装运延误以及因此造成的所有不便表示歉意。

3. in receipt of : having received/in possession of   收到，接到

We are in receipt of a letter of complaint.

我们已收到一封投诉信。

We are in receipt of your enquiry dated Oct. 15th.

我们已收到贵方 10 月 15 日询盘。

on/upon receipt of 一收到……就

Shipment will be effected on/upon receipt of your L/C.

一收到信用证即安排装运。

4. on the basis of

We are establishing business relations on the basis of equality and mutual benefit.

我们在平等互利的基础上建立业务关系。

Please quote us your most competitive prices for the following goods on the basis of CIF London.

请报以下产品最具竞争性的伦敦到岸价。

We hope you can agree to ship the goods to us as before on the basis of Cash Against Documents.

我们希望你们能像以前那样在交单付现的基础上运送货物。

Expressions

For proposal of favorable payment terms

1. We shall be glad if you agree to ship the goods on … basis.

2. We hope you will accommodate us in this respect and accept …terms.

3. In consideration of …, we propose that you would be in agreement to…

For stating the reasons of asking for favorable payment terms

1. Because our funds are tied up, we would like to…

2. As the tie-up of funds indeed presents a problem to us, please…

3. Because of the tight money condition and high bank interest, it is hard for us to make purchase on …basis.

Part III
Practical Writing

Main Information

🍀 Practice 1

Complete the following chart according to Sample 1.

Buyer's favorable payment terms: _____

Reasons: _____

Key Phrases

🍀 Practice 2

Translate the following phrases into Chinese or English.

English	Chinese
for/in the amount of	_____
make/effect payment	_____
D/P (Documents against Payment)	_____
D/A (Documents against Acceptance)	_____
finalize/conclude/close a transaction	_____
_____	搁置资金
_____	收到
_____	宽松的付款方式
_____	以……为基础
_____	保兑的不可撤销信用证

🍀 Practice 3

Complete the following sentences with the proper form of the words or phrases given in the box.

in agreement to	accommodate	involve	exceed	financial standing
request	payment terms	refer to	in response to	settle

1. The _____ for easier terms of payment is compelled by their funds being tied up.

2. As to our _____ , you can check it with the Bank of China, Shanghai Branch.

3. We are _____ your proposal and accept terms of payment by D/A.

4. We note from your letter of June 6 that you wish to have a change in _____ .

5. We hope you will extend us a special _____ and agree to D/P terms.

6. Since the amount _____ is rather small, we suggest you accept payment on collection basis.

7. If the amount _____ that figure, payment by L/C will be required.

8. _____ your request, we shall do business with you with D/A terms.

9. International traders often request a longer period for _____ of an account.

10. We _____ the men's T-shirts under Contract No.123 in the amount of $5,000.

Useful Expressions

Practice 4

Complete the following sentences in English.

1. We have confidence in 在本地市场促销你公司产品 . (push sales of)

　　　　　　为贵方获得大订单 . (obtain)

　　　　　　促进双方业务的发展 . (facilitate)

2. For this transaction, we propose 以六十天远期信用证付款 . (payment)

　　　　　　贵方以托收方式交货 . (regular order)

　　　　　　贵方同意付款交单条款 . (agree to)

3. Needless to say, we much appreciate 你们的友好合作 . (friendly)

　　　　　　你们过去对我们的支持 . (support)

　　　　　　贵方给我们的特殊照顾 . (accommodation)

Practice 5

Rewrite the underlined parts in the letter below with two different expressions but without changing the meaning of the sentences.

Dear Sirs,

　　We refer to your Contract No. 456 covering men's shoes in the amount of $5,000.

　　①We note from your letter of July 6 that you insist on payment by irrevocable L/C .

　　②Since the amount involved in this transaction is small, we shall be glad if you agree to ship the goods to us on D/P basis. Taking our long business relationship into consideration, ③we hope you will give us a special accommodation in this respect.

　　We look forward to receiving your early and favorable reply.

Yours faithfully,

① We note from your letter of July 6 that you insist on payment by irrevocable L/C

a. _____

b. _____

② Since the amount involved in this transaction is small

a. _____

b. _____

③ we hope you will give us a special accommodation in this respect

a. _____

b. _____

Letter Writing

🍀 Practice 6

Compose a letter asking for D/A payment with the following information.

① the accommodation will be beneficial to both sides

② we have successfully finalized the transaction of 1,000 bicycles

③ we can further push the sales of your products here

④ you will do us a favor and exceptionally accept D/A terms

⑤ we are operating in a very competitive market

June 6, 2011

Dear Sirs,

Thanks to your close cooperation, _____. Our customers show great interest in your products. We feel confident that _____.

As you know, _____. To lure big buyers and superstores, many local and international suppliers are offering easier payment terms. Therefore, we hope _____. We are sure _____.

We look forward to your early and favorable response.

Yours faithfully,

🍀 Practice 7

Write a letter asking for D/A payment according to the information below.

Owing to the promising market in your local area, you will place an order for 1,000 Sony digital cameras with Mayflower Co. Ltd. In the letter of Oct. 10 the seller ask for payment by L/C, but you think payment by L/C will tie up funds for three or four months. Write a letter to the seller asking for D/A payment.

Practice 8

Complete the reply to the letter of Practice 7 according to the Chinese in the parentheses.

Dear Sirs,

    We are in possession of your letter of October 16 and are glad to learn that you have made great efforts to push the sales of our Sony digital cameras in your market.

    Although we highly appreciate your efforts to help sell our products, ①_____

_____(但对你们要求承兑交单付款一事，我们歉难考虑). It is clearly stipulated in the contract that payment should be made by confirmed, irrevocable L/C payable by sight draft.

    However, in view of our long friendly business relations, ②_____

_____ (我方乐意接受即期付款交单付款方式，以示特别照顾).

    ③_____ (希望贵方接受上述条款) and look forward to your early reply.

Yours sincerely,

Part IV
Supplementary Reading

Reading One

Dear Sir or Madam,

    Reference is made to our Contract No. 668 covering 100 washing machines in the amount of 30,000 dollars.

    As regards the payment terms, we hope you will make an exception and accept D/A or D/P terms. Payment by L/C is more complicated and expensive. When we apply to open an L/C with a bank, we have to pay a sum of deposit. This will add to the cost of our imports and also tie up our money. Moreover, we have to pay bank charges for opening the L/C, which will further increase the cost of what we import.

    We shall appreciate your accommodation in this respect. We can assure you that if D/A terms are acceptable and this transaction turns out to our satisfaction, substantial orders will follow.

    We await your early reply.

Yours sincerely,

Reading Two

Dear Sir or Madam,

Thanks to your close cooperation, we have successfully concluded a deal for 2,000 pairs of women's casual shoes. We have noted your request for D/A payment in your letter dated June 20, but we regret that we are unable to accept it.

Payment by L/C is a common practice in international business. When dealing with a new customer, we usually require payment by confirmed, irrevocable L/C. However, as the business between us increases, we will consider granting you easier payment terms and accept D/P payment. But, for now, we insist on payment by sight L/C.

We wish to point out that you make sure the stipulations in the L/C are in full compliance with those in the S/C to ensure the smooth execution of the contract.

Thank you very much for your understanding and support.

Yours sincerely,

Lesson Ten ●●●

Urging Establishment of L/C

Objectives

To be proficient in
◎ understanding the main information and key terms often used in a letter of urging establishment of L/C
◎ writing a letter of urging establishment of L/C

Writing Tips

L/C is the most generally used method of payment in international trade. A letter urging the establishment of an L/C aims to persuade the buyers to cooperate more closely and fulfill their obligations. Therefore, letters urging the establishment of an L/C must be written with tact, that is, the letter should not strongly blame the buyer for his failure to open the relative L/C in time, but in a polite way.

Part I
Warm-up Activities

◆ **Write out at least four parties involved in payment by L/C in international trade.**

④

①

Payment by L/C

③

②

◆ **Please arrange the following steps involved in payment by L/C in the correct order.**

① Applying for the issuance of L/C ④ Negotiating the L/C

② Signing a contract payment by L/C ⑤ Issuing the L/C

③ Checking the L/C then shipping the goods ⑥ Advising the L/C

Part II
Sample Study

Sample 1

June 16, 2011

Dear Sir or Madam,

We wish to inform you that the goods under our S/C No 2567 have been ready for shipment for quite some time. It is stipulated in the *foregoing* S/C that shipment is to be made during July and the L/C should reach the seller at least one month before shipment.

But much to our *disappointment*, we have not yet received any news of L/C from you. As the shipment date is approaching, it is *imperative* that you take immediate action to have the relevant credit established without delay. Otherwise, any losses caused by delay of shipment shall be *for your account*. If your L/C fails to reach us by the end of this month, we *have no choice but to* cancel your order.

We shall be pleased if you give prompt attention to this matter and open the L/C with the least possible delay.

Your cooperation in this regard will be highly appreciated.

Yours sincerely,

Sample 2

July 23, 2011

Dear Sir or Madam,

Thank you for your letter of July 16. As requested, the L/C in question has already been opened and sent.

For your reference, we are enclosing a copy of Documentary Credit No 156, covering the 500 color TVs for the amount of 260,000 dollars. Please contact your bank to check the relevant L/C.

As our customers are in *urgent* need of the above mentioned goods, we shall be obliged if you could make an immediate response and effect prompt shipment. Would you please kindly let us know *at your earliest convenience* the name and sailing date of the carrying vessel?

Your favorable reply shall be highly appreciated.

Yours sincerely,

Vocabulary

foregoing	/'fɔːgəʊɪŋ/	*a.* 在前的，前述的
disappointment	/ˌdɪsə'pɔɪntmənt/	*n.* 失望，沮丧，扫兴
imperative	/ɪm'perətɪv/	*a.* 必要的，迫切的
urgent	/'ɜːdʒənt/	*a.* 十分重要的；紧急的
for your account		在……账上，费用由……承担
have no choice but to		别无他法，别无选择，只好
at your earliest convenience		得便务请……，尽早

Notes

1. for one's account: at one's cost/ expense   在……账上，费用由……承担

If you hope to have the goods insured against All Risks, we can comply with your request. But the extra premium shall be for your account.

如果贵方希望投保一切险，我们将满足你方需求，但额外的保险费应由贵方承担。

on account of: because of 由于

On account of the low stock of such goods, we would advise you to accept our quotation immediately.

由于我们近来货源不足，我们建议贵方尽快接受我们的报价。

take account of / take... into account 考虑到……，顾及……

Would you please take our long business relationship into account and accept our proposal of D/A payment terms?

请考虑我们之间长期的业务关系，接受我方提议的承兑交单付款方式。

2. have no choice but to: have to

She had no choice but to leave his company.

除了离开公司，她别无选择。

Unless you can reduce your quotations, we shall have no choice but to buy elsewhere.

如果贵方不能降低报价，我们只好从其他销售商处购买。

As you failed to make delivery in time, we have no choice but to cancel our order with you.

因为贵方没有按时交货，我们别无选择，只好取消订单。

3. in urgent need of: in great need of 急需

Our customers are in urgent need of the captioned goods.

我们的客户急需上述货物。

The users are in urgent need of the machines contracted and are in fact pressing us for an early delivery.

用户急需合同项下的机器，并催促我们早日装船。

The management system is in urgent need of reform.

管理体制急需改革。

Expressions

For complaining about non-receipt of L/C

1. We regret to say that your L/C has not reached us till now.

2. We have not received any information from you about your L/C which should reach us…

3. We have not received your relevant L/C up to now.

For asking for opening the L/C

1. It would be advisable for you to establish the covering L/C as early as possible.

2. We expect your L/C to be established immediately.

3. Please do your utmost to expedite the issue of the relevant L/C.

For inviting attention to the matter

1. We wish to draw your attention to the fact that…

2. Your prompt attention in this regard will be highly appreciated.

3. Please give this matter your immediate attention.

Part III
Practical Writing

Main Information

Practice 1

Complete the following chart according to Sample 1.

Complaint about non-receipt of L/C: _____

Requirements: _____

Consequences of L/C failing to reach on time: _____

Key Phrases

♣ Practice 2

Translate the following phrases into Chinese or English.

English	Chinese
up to the present/up to now/ till now	_____
in one's favor	_____
issue/ establish/open an L/C	_____
documentary credit	_____
for one's account	_____
_____	急需
_____	备妥待运
_____	装运日期
_____	只好
_____	装运

♣ Practice 3

Complete the following sentences with the proper form of the words or phrases given in the box below.

establish	apply	urge	approach	for one's account
favor	for the amount of	accept	recommend	receive

1. We _____ that you open the L/C with the least possible delay.

2. Please have your L/C _____ and let us have your reply by return.

3. Two weeks ago, we sent you an email _____ the establishment of the relative L/C.

4. As the date of shipment is approaching, please _____ for the establishment of L/C.

5. Needless to say, we won't deliver the goods unless we _____ your L/C as agreed.

6. We have issued an irrevocable L/C in your _____.

7. The sales season is _____ and your skirts are in great demand.

8. We have not received your L/C issued by HSBC _____ $8,000.

9. If your L/C doesn't reach us as required, extra charges arising from this will be _____.

10. If the above terms and conditions are _____ to you, please send us a letter at your earliest convenience.

Useful Expressions

♣ Practice 4

Complete the following sentences in English.

1. We shall be obliged if 贵方早日开立信用证. (establish)

   贵方加速装运我方的货物. (expedite)

   贵方立即对此事予以关注. (attention)

2. We would like to point out that 贵方信用证未按时到达我方. (reach)

   延期装运将给我方带来巨大损失. (cause)

   信用证规定事项必须与合同条款一致. (in accordance with)

3. We regret to say that 贵方信用证至今未到，这给我们带来极大不便. (inconvenience)

   由于有关信用证延期到达，我们无法在规定时限内装运货物. (late arrival)

   因我方未按时收到贵方信用证无法履行合同. (execute)

♣ Practice 5

Rewrite the underlined parts in the letter below with two different expressions, but without changing the meaning of the sentences.

Dear Sirs,

   We refer to the goods under Contract No.236, which have been ready for quite some time. However, ①we would like to point out that the covering L/C has not reached us so far. ② It is imperative that you take immediate action and have the L/C established as soon as possible.

   In spite of our repeated requests, we still have not received the relative L/C as of writing. As the shipment date is approaching, we won't ship the goods unless your L/C reaches us on time. ③The losses arising from delays in shipment shall be for your account.

   We hope you will pay prompt attention to this matter and look forward to your early reply.

Yours faithfully,

① we would like to point out that the covering L/C has not reached us so far

   a. _____

   b. _____

② It is imperative that you take immediate action and have the L/C established as soon as possible

   a. _____

   b. _____

③ The losses arising from delays in shipment shall be for your account

   a. _____

   b. _____

Letter Writing

♣ Practice 6

Compose a letter urging establishment of L/C with the following information.

① have the relative L/C established with the least possible delay

② the L/C stipulations are in exact accordance with the terms set forth in our contract

③ you will be responsible for all losses arising from delays in shipment

④ the relative L/C has not reached us at this time

⑤ the goods have been ready for shipment for quite some time

May 15, 2011

Dear Sirs,

In reference to the 1,000 electric fans under Contract No. 254, _____.
However, we regret to say that _____.

Although we have sent you an email one week ago pressing for opening the L/C, we have not received any reply yet. Please give this matter your immediate attention and _____. Otherwise, _____.

When establishing the L/C, please see to it that _____.

Your cooperation in this regard will be appreciated.

Yours faithfully,

♣ Practice 7

Write a letter of urging establishment of L/C according to the information below.

You are a leading producer and exporter of massage chairs. Recently you have successfully concluded a transaction of 1,000 massage chairs with the Star International Trade Corporation. According to the contract, the relative L/C should reach you before August, but you still have not yet received the L/C till August 14. As the goods are ready for shipment, please write a letter to the buyer urging them to establish the covering L/C immediately.

♣ Practice 8

Complete the reply to the letter of Practice 7 according to the Chinese in the parentheses.

Dear Sir or Madam,

Thank you for your letter of August 16. ①_____ (很高兴告知贵方相关信用证已由中国银行开出)，who enjoys a high credit standing.

We are glad to learn that the goods we ordered have been ready for shipment. ②_____ (如告知船名和启航日期，我方将不胜感激).

③_____ (期待贵方即刻装运).

Yours sincerely,

Part IV Supplementary Reading

Reading One

Dear Sir or Madam,

We refer to our Sales Contract No. 865. Under the terms of the contract, delivery is to be made during September, but the covering L/C has not reached us yet.

A week ago, we sent you an e-mail to remind you that the delivery date is approaching and urge you to arrange your bank to open the relative L/C immediately. But so far, we have had no response.

We wish to point out that the goods have been ready for some time and direct steamers from here to your port are far few and between. We are informed by the local shipping company that S.S Sunshine is due to sail at the beginning of September. If we miss this steamer, we might not find another before the end of September. Please open the relative L/C without delay. Otherwise, you shall be responsible for any losses arising from this.

We look forward to your early reply.

Yours sincerely,

Reading Two

Dear Sir or Madam,

Thank you for your letter dated August 11. We have the pleasure of informing you that L/C No. 489 for the amount of $ 50,000 has been established in your favor through the Hong Kong and Shanghai Banking Corporation, New York Branch. If everything goes smoothly, it will be in your possession next week.

As you know, the time of delivery is a matter of great importance to us. October is the peak sales season for this commodity in our market. If we can not place our goods in the market at that time, we shall suffer great loss.

Therefore, we shall be grateful if you could arrange shipment immediately after receiving the L/C.

Thank you for your cooperation.

Yours sincerely,

Lesson Eleven •●●

Asking for Amendment to L/C

Objectives

To be proficient in

◎ understanding the main information and key terms used in a letter of asking for amendment to L/C

◎ writing a letter of asking for amendment to L/C

Writing Tips

On receiving the relevant L/C, the exporter should first make a full examination to see whether the clauses set forth in the L/C are in compliance with the terms stated in the sales contract. If any discrepancies between the L/C and Sales Contract are found, the exporter will ask the importer to make an amendment.

Here are some guidelines:

● thank for opening the L/C;

● tell the discrepancies between the L/C and the contract;

● show the requirements for amendments;

● expect punctual amendments.

Part I
Warm-up Activities

◆ Discuss in groups and tell what clauses may be amended in an L/C.

intensedebate

◆ Correct the errors underlined in the L/C according to the contract below.

Contract No. 248B

......

Unit price: at USD 250 per M/T CIF London

Total Value: USD 50,000 (Say US Dollars Fifty Thousand Only)

Insurance: To be covered by the seller against All Risks and War Risk for 110% of the invoice value

---

HSBC London Branch

Irrevocable Documentary Credit

No. LSP 156

......

Amount: ①USD 65,000 (Say Sixty-five Thousand Dollars Only)

Credit available against presentation of the following documents and of your draft at sight for 100% of the invoice value:

......

-One original marine insurance policy for ②130% full invoice value covering All Risks and War Risk Covering 200 M/T Dongbei Rice, first grade, at USD 250 per M/T ③CFR London as per Contract No. 248B

......

Part II
Sample Study

Sample 1

Dear Sir or Madam,

    With reference to the 1,000 metric tons of wheat under our S/C NO.126, we find that there are several points in the L/C not *in accordance with* what *stipulated* in the contract, so please *amend* the L/C as follows:

- The value of your L/C is *insufficient*. The total value is US$3, 200 instead of US$3,000;
- Please add the wording: "3% more or less allowed" after the number of the quantity;
- The L/C should be valid until the fifteenth day after shipment.

    We would like you to make the above-mentioned amendments without delay so that we can book *shipping space* in time.

    Your early reply will be highly appreciated.

Yours sincerely,

Sample 2

Dear Sir or Madam,

    Letter of Credit No. 3324 *issued* by the Bank of New South Wales has arrived. *On perusal*, we find that transshipment and partial shipment are not allowed.

    As direct steamers to your port are *few and far between, more often than not* we have to ship via Hong Kong. As to partial shipment, it would be to our mutual benefit if we could ship in 2 lots instead of waiting for the whole shipment to be completed. Therefore, we are asking you to amend your L/C to read "Partial shipments and transshipment allowed."

    We shall appreciate it if you will promptly *modify* the L/C as requested.

Yours sincerely,

Vocabulary

stipulate   /'stɪpjʊleɪt/   *v.* 规定；制定要求

amend	/ə'mend/	v. 修改；改善，改正
insufficient	/ˌɪnsə'fɪʃnt/	a. 不足的，不够的
issue	/'ɪʃuː/	v. 发行；分发；发送
modify	/'mɒdɪfaɪ/	v. 修改，修饰；更改
in accordance with		与……一致
shipping space		舱位
on perusal		经详阅
few and far between		稀少；彼此相距很远；不常发生
more often than not		通常，多半

 Notes

1. in accordance with: in conformity with

in exact/full accordance with 与……完全一致

The quality of the goods should be in accordance with that of the sample.

货物的质量应与样品质量保持一致。

Each production procedure of the company is in accordance with the ISO900 system.

公司的每道生产工序应该遵循 ISO900 认证体系。

To prepare monthly plan of construction capital, we make the payment in accordance with the daily plan.

编制基建资金月度用款计划，按日计划办理付款。

2. stipulate

stipulate in explicit terms   明文规定

stipulate a commission rate   规定代理费

The company fails to pay on the date stipulated in the contract.

该公司没有按合同中规定的日期付款。

Can you stipulate that they would carry out the contract?

你能保证他们会执行该合同吗？

The contract stipulates that the seller pays the buyer's legal cost.

合同规定卖方支付买方的诉讼费用。

3. amend

We have to ask you to amend the relevant L/C according to the contract terms.

我们必须要求贵方按照合同条款修改相关信用证。

Please amend the shipment in your L/C to read "Partial shipment and transshipment allowed".

请贵方将信用证中的装运条款修改为"允许分批装运和转运"。

It's your responsibility to draft, make, amend, and check the internal managerial regulations and systems.

起草、制定、修改、审核内部管理规章制度是你的责任。

4. insufficient

insufficient justification 理由不足效应；理由不足

insufficient fund 存款不足；金额不足

The amount of your L/C is insufficient, which will lead to much trouble for both sides.

贵方的信用证资金不足，这会给双方带来许多麻烦。

We have received your L/C dated October 8 and found that the amount is insufficient.

我方收到贵方 10 月 8 日的信用证，发现金额不足。

The claim that the crisis was due to insufficient regulation was also unconvincing.

危机是由于监管不够的说法也站不住脚。

5. on perusal: on examination

On perusal, we found several discrepancies on your presented documents.

经详阅，我方发现与贵方所提供的单据有些差异。

On perusal, we found the goods don't conform to the original sample.

经详阅，我方发现货物与样品不相符。

On perusal, we found that part of the content did not conform to the original contract.

经过审查，我们发现部分内容与原合同不符。

6. few and far between 稀少

We have to wait for another 10 days to ship the goods, because the direct sailing to your port is few and far between.

因为达到贵方港口的直达轮很少，我方不得不又等待 10 天才能装运货物。

Because direct steamers to your port are few and far between, we should transship via Hong Kong.

由于到你处的直达轮很少，所以我们必须在香港转运。

7. more often than not

Their client is more often than not the Algerian state.

他们的客户经常是阿尔及利亚政府。

More often than not the international investment community tends to discount political and business connections.

越来越多的国际投资团体趋向于不看重政治和商务的联系。

Expressions

For receiving the L/C

1. We have received your L/C No. …

2. Thank you for your L/C No. …

3. We thank you for your letters of credit No. …

4. We are in receipt of your letter of …

For asking for amendment to L/C

1. We have received your relative L/C, but to our regret that it contains the following discrepancies…

2. Much to our regret, we find that there is no stipulation of transshipment being allowed in the relative L/C, so…

3. The Bill of Lading should be marked "Freight Collect" instead of "Freight Prepaid".

4. Please amend L/C No.125 to read "This L/C will expire on July 24".

For expecting an early amendment

1. Your prompt attention to the matter would be much appreciated.

2. If the amendments to the L/C come too late, we will not be able to ship the goods in time.

3. Please amend your L/C as soon as possible in order to enable us to effect shipment.

4. We hope you will see to it that the amendment is made without delay.

Part III
Practical Writing

Main Information

♣ Practice 1

Complete the following chart according to Sample 1.

Importer: _____

Intention: _____

Discrepancies: _____

Requirements: _____

Key Phrases

♣ Practice 2

Translate the following phrases into Chinese or English.

English	Chinese
partial shipment	_____
on perusal	_____
few and far between	_____
shipping space	
direct steamer	
_____	与……相一致，根据
_____	通常，多半
_____	按照要求

_____

_____

或多或少

修改……如下

◆ Practice 3

Complete the following sentences with the proper form of the words or phrases given in the box below.

regret	insert	discrepancy	on perusal	amend	insufficient
read	overdue	prohibit	convenience	stipulate	validity

1. It appears that the _____ in the L/C are not in agreement with the contract.

2. Please _____ the word "about" before the amount in your L/C No. 126.

3. After checking it carefully, we regret to say that we have found some _____.

4. We look forward to receiving the relevant _____ at an early date.

5. The amount in your L/C appears _____. Please increase the amount by $800.

6. _____, we find the price does not conform to that in the contract.

7. We will appreciate it if you give us response at the earliest _____.

8. Please amend the clause to read "Transshipment is _____".

9. We reluctantly ask you to amend your L/C to _____: Partial shipment.

10. As the deadline for the contract will soon be _____, please make the necessary amendments.

Useful Expressions

◆ Practice 4

Complete the following sentences in English.

1. It was stipulated that 卖方必须在合同时间内装运 . (effect shipment)

   该产品须在六日内送交 . (deliver)

2. We regret to say that 信用证条款中两点与合同不符 . (conform to)

   发现有一些差异 . (discrepancy)

3. Please amend 你方信用证允许转船和分批装运 . (transshipment and partial shipment)

   信用证的受益人改为"南方贸易公司". (beneficiary of the L/C South Trading Company)

◆ Practice 5

Rewrite the underlined parts in the letter below with two different expressions, but without changing the meaning of the sentences.

Dear Sir,

①Thank you for your L/C No. 6688 covering your order for 1,000 cartons of dinner sets. ②On perusal, we find that partial shipment and transshipment are not allowed.

We regret to say that we have only 600 cartons of goods available so far and the remaining 400 cartons will not be ready until the end of next month. Moreover we would like you to know that there is no direct steamer from Tianjin to your port during the current two months.

③Such being the case, we would request you to amend your L/C to allow partial shipment and transshipment so that we can immediately ship whatever we have on hand via Hong Kong.

④We hope you will see to it that amendment should be made without delay.

Yours faithfully,

① Thank you for your L/C No.6688 covering your order for 1,000 cartons of dinner sets

a. _____

b. _____

② On perusal, we find that partial shipment and transshipment are not allowed

a. _____

b. _____

③ Such being the case, we would ask you to amend your L/C to allow partial shipment and transshipment

a. _____

b. _____

④ We hope you will see to it that amendment should be made without delay

a. _____

b. _____

Letter Writing

♣ Practice 6

Compose a letter of asking for amendment to the L/C with the given information.

① although the word is clearly indicated in our S/C

② We have received with thanks your L/C No. 6422

③ shipment should be effected in two equal monthly lots

④ make the necessary amendments immediately

⑤ your L/C will allow transshipment

⑥ in order to make us effect shipment

Dear Sirs,

_____ established against the S/C No. NH888, but, much to our regret, there are some discrepancies between the L/C and the S/C. We list them as follows:

- It is stipulated in S/C No. NH888 that _____, but the L/C in hand states "TRANSSHIPMENT PROHIBITED".
- Our S/C states clearly: "Shipment is to be made in a single lot not later than September 30" whereas your L/C No. 6422 says that _____ during August and September.
- There is no word "about" before the quantity and amount in the L/C, _____.

We would like you to _____. As you know, shipment will not be made until the above amendments are corrected.

Please amend your L/C as soon as possible _____.

Yours faithfully

♣ Practice 7

Write a letter of asking for amendment to L/C according to the information given below.

★ Receive the L/C No. 1886 and find the discrepancies

★ Amendments:

The quantity is 60 cases instead of 80 cases

Insert "about" before the quantity

Partial shipment and transshipment allowed

Validity to be extended to 10th November

♣ Practice 8

Complete the reply to the letter of Practice 7 according to the Chinese in the parentheses.

Dear Sirs,

We have received your letter of June 23 requesting us to amend the L/C No. 1886. We regret that some of the clauses are not in conformity with the contract. ① _____
_____ （经详阅，我们同意信用证修改如下）:

- Insert a word "about" before the quantity.
- ② _____ （同意分批装运和转船）.
- ③ _____ （数量减少至60箱）.
- Amend the validity to 10th November.

④ _____ （感谢贵方的密切合作）.

Yours sincerely,

Part IV
Supplementary Reading

Reading One

Dear Sirs,

We have duly received your letter of credit No. 1226 issued by the Bank of New York. However, on examination, we are sorry to find it includes the following items which are not in agreement with our Sales Contract No. AC3846. Please make amendments to it:

1. We request you to amend "Transshipment and partial shipment are not allowed" to read "Transshipment and partial shipment are allowed".

The reason why we make this amendment is that direct sailing to your port is few and far this season, so we have to ship via Hong Kong. As to partial shipment, it can help us arrange to make shipment immediately so that you can catch a market share.

2. Expiry date should be July 23 and the period of presenting documents should be within 10 days after shipment.

3. Place of expiry should be in Guangzhou, China. The advising or negotiating bank should be the Bank of China, Guangzhou Branch.

4. Increase the amount by USD1, 000.

Please amend your L/C as soon as possible in order to enable us to effect shipment.

Yours sincerely,

Reading Two

Dear Sir or Madam,

We thank you for your letter of credit No. 0128, but we find that it contains the following discrepancies:

1. The commission granted for this transaction should be 2%, but your L/C requests a commission of 6%.

2. The shipment should be effected during July, instead of "on or before 30 June".

3. Please amend the above L/C to read piece length in 20 yards instead of 30 yards.

4. Please pay attention to the fact that the specification of our goods is 35 × 35 and 75 × 60 whereas your credit calls for 30 × 30 and 75 × 60.

Therefore, please amend the credit according to the stipulation of the contract.

If your amendment could reach us by the end of this month, we would make shipment in the first half of next month.

Yours sincerely,

Unit 5

Shipment and Insurance

Packing Instruction

Objectives

To be proficient in

◎ understanding the main information and key terms often used in a letter of packing instruction

◎ writing a letter of packing instruction

Writing Tips

Packing is very important in international trade. The product will need packing no matter whatever mode of transport is used. In recent years, the significance of packing has been increasingly recognized because packing is a main force in the fierce market competition and packing is also an important component of the description of goods and a main item of a sale contract or a Letter of Credit. Packing can be usually divided into two types: out packing and inner packing.

Here are some guidelines:

● Express the purpose of the letter, i.e. negotiating on packing;

● Specify the packing requirements, such as packing ways, packing materials etc.;

● Indicate your expectation and desire.

Part I
Warm-up Activities

◆ **Translate the following marks into Chinese.**

_____

_____

_____

◆ **Give more marks after discussing with your partner.**

Part II
Sample Study

Sample 1

Dear Sir or Madam,

With reference to our Order No. 3018 for 100 cardboard cartons of beer glasses to be shipped to us during August, as the items are highly *fragile*, please *see to* it that the goods must be *packed* according to our instruction lest they are damaged *in transit*.

We would like to have beer glasses packed half dozen in a box, 8 boxes in a carton, 2 cartons in a wooden case. The boxes are to *be padded with* foamed plastic. Apart from this, we hope the inner packing will be attractive and helpful to the sales while the outer packing is strong enough to *withstand* rough handling and the sea transportation. *Warning marks* as

"Handle with Care" should also appear on the outer packing so as to avoid any *negligence* that causes unexpected trouble and expense.

We hope our goods will arrive in perfect condition.

Yours sincerely,

Sample 2

Dear Sir or Madam,

We have received your e-mail dated March 12 with many thanks.

Enclosed is our Order No. 316 placed US$1,200 per set CFR Sydney for 100 sets of HDTV.

For this is the first trade between us, we would like to say *in advance* that one TV set is packed in a cardboard box, 4 sets to a wooden case *lined with* water proof material and bound with two iron straps outside. Please pay attention to the fact that the cases should be strong enough to prevent the items from any unexpected damage in transit. *Shipping marks* are *stenciled* on the outer packing , as shown below:

ACCED

NO.316

Sydney

No.1-25

If it is acceptable to you, please let us know as soon as possible.

Yours sincerely,

Vocabulary

fragile	/'frædʒaɪl/	a. 易碎的；脆的
pack	/pæk/	v. 包装
withstand	/wɪð'stænd/	v. 抵挡，禁得起，抵抗
negligence	/'neglɪdʒəns/	n. 疏忽；忽视；粗心大意
stencil	/'stensl/	v. 用模板印刷（图案），刷唛
see to		务必（使），注意（使）
in transit		运输途中，运送中
be padded with		用……作为垫
warning marks		警示标志
in advance		事先，提前
(be) lined with		用……作为内衬
shipping mark		装运标记，箱唛

Notes

1. fragile

fragile products 易碎品

It is also a crucial question for the fragile global economy.

对于脆弱的全球经济而言，这个问题同样关键。

But the fallout from a collapse in the mortgage and lending markets could shake fragile consumers' confidence further.

然而，抵押和贷款市场崩盘的影响可能会进一步动摇本已脆弱的消费者信心。

2. see to 务必（使），注意（使）

The packing condition is out of order, and the boss will see to it.

包装状况混乱，老板将进行处理。

Please see to it that the L/C terms should be in accordance with those in the contract.

请注意信用证条款必须与合同条款一致。

Please see to it that the goods should reach here two weeks before the selling season.

请注意，商品必须在销售季节前两周到达。

Please see to it that the packing is strong enough to withstand rough handling.

请务必做到包装牢固，经得起粗鲁搬运。

3. pack

packing *n.* 包装

inner packing 内包装

outer packing 外包装

sales packing 销售包装

shipping packing 运输包装

packing list 装箱单

包装表达常用介词：

1）in… 用某种容器包装

Walnuts are to be packed in double gunny bags.

花生要用双层麻袋包装。

2）…to… 若干件装于一种容器中

Our trip knives are packed in boxes, 50 boxes to a carton.

旅行小刀用盒装，50 盒装于 1 木箱。

3）in…of…each 用某种容器包装，每件内装若干。

Jackets are packed in ploy bags of 10 pieces each.

夹克用塑料袋包装，每 10 件装 1 袋。

4）…to…and …to… 若干单位装某种容器，若干此种容器装于另一较大的容器

Pencils are packed 12 pieces to a box and 300 boxes to a carton.

每一打铅笔装 1 盒，300 盒装 1 纸箱。

4. in transit

The cargo was damaged in transit.

货物在运输途中受损。

Perishable goods are subject to damage in transit.

易腐烂的货物在运输中容易损坏。

Please give special attention to the packing, or the goods could be damaged in transit.

请特别注意包装，否则，货物可能会在运输中遭损。

5. withstand

By then, it is hoped, the economy will be strong enough to withstand it.

希望到那时，经济能够足够强大，能承受该项计划实施所带来的压力。

Big companies have more power to negotiate with suppliers and are better able to withstand the industry's cycle.

在与供应商谈判时，大型公司可以掌握更多的话语权，同时大型公司还可以很好地承受产业周期变化所带来的冲击。

EARLIER this year most businessmen and investors hoped that Asia's emerging economies could withstand the economic and financial turmoil in the developed world.

今年年初，多数企业家和投资者都希望亚洲新兴经济体能成功抵御源于发达国家的经济危机。

6. negligence

Because of his negligence, the goods were damaged in transit.

由于他的疏忽大意，货物在运输中受损。

Ignorance and negligence has caused this mistake.

无知与疏忽是这错误的原因。

The drawee or his agent who makes payment out of ill intention or with gross negligence shall bear liability on his own.

付款人及其代理付款人恶意付款或者付款重大过失，应当自行承担责任。

7. in advance 事先，提前

No interest shall be deducted from the principal in advance.

利息不得预先在本金中扣除。

But at least most of these estimates were agreed in advance.

但至少其中大部分估价都是事先约定好的。

If his boss breaches in 3 days in advance, he will charge 80% of the total rental rate.

如果他的老板提前 3 天以下解除协议，他将支付租金总额 80%的违约金。

Because our supply of raw materials has been committed to other clients for months in advance, we cannot accept your order at present.

因为我方的原料供应在几个月前已分配给其他客户，故目前不能接受贵公司的订单。

8. stencil

Stencil an address on a packing case.

用模板在包装箱上印刷地址。

Don't forget to stencil the shipping marks on the outer packing.

请别忘了在外包装刷唛。

Please stencil the bales with our design in strict accordance with our instruction.

请严格按照说明刷上我公司提供的图样。

 ## Expressions

For offering packing requirements

1. With reference to the packing of our Order No. 128 for…

2. We are very glad to advise you of the packing method of …

3. We are now referring to the packing of

4. We are writing to you in regard to the packing of…

For specifying the packing requirements

1. The packing clause is as follows:

2. The packing should …

3. The shipping marks should be …

4. We would like you to have the goods packed in …

For indicating your expectation and desire

1. It would be highly appreciated if you let us know your ideas on the packing requirements.

2. Kindly inform us your opinions about the above mentioned issue of packing.

3. We hope that you will find the packing arrangement to your convenience and satisfaction.

4. Please tell us whether the packing requirement is satisfactory.

Part III
Practical Writing

Main Information

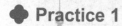 ### Practice 1

Complete the following chart according to Sample 1.

Importer: _____

Intention: _____

Requirements: _____

Key Phrases

♣ Practice 2

Translate the following phrases into Chinese or English.

English	Chinese
be padded with	_____
see to	_____
shipping mark	_____
in advance	_____
in transit	_____
_____	警示标志
_____	用……作为内衬
_____	易碎品
_____	装箱单
_____	内包装

♣ Practice 3

Complete the following sentences with the proper form of the words or phrases given in the box below.

pack	in transit	withstand	line	stencil
reinforce	adopt	negligence	container	see to

1. You can rest assured that all the cartons are _____ plastic sheets, so they are absolutely water proof.

2. The packing should be strong enough to _____ rough handling.

3. We will take every step within our reach to improve the _____ so as to protect the goods from breakage.

4. We believe such packing will reduce any possible damage _____ to a minimum.

5. Taking into consideration the transport at your end, we have especially _____ our packing.

6. The newly-_____ style of packing is specially designed to suit the young's taste.

7. Please _____ our initials and order numbers on the outer packing.

8. Our _____ are in conformity with the specification stipulated by the International Standardization Organization.

9. Owing to the _____ of packing staff, the items are not wrapped with shake-proof materials.

10. Please _____ it that the packing of the goods shall be in compliance with that stipulated in the contract.

Useful Expressions

♣ Practice 4

Complete the following sentences in English.

1. The items are packed 每件套一个塑料袋，每5打装有防水衬里 . (in…to…)
   用双层帆布袋 .（canvas bags）

2. On the outer packing, please 刷上三角形，三角形内标上我公司的缩写字母 . (stencil)
   标明："小心轻放"、"易燃品"等字样 .

3. Each carton 衬防水材料，以防内装货物受潮 . (be lined with)
   垫泡沫塑料，以防内装货物因粗暴搬运而引起损坏 . (be padded with)

♣ Practice 5

Rewrite the underlined parts in the letter below with two different expressions, but without changing the meaning of the sentences.

Dear Sirs,

①With reference to the packing of our Order No. 135 for 1,000 cases of Australian wines, we hope to call your attention to the fact that the goods are easy to break during the course of transportation. Therefore, ②we suggest that the Australian wines be packed in seaworthy cases capable of withstanding rough handling. On the outer packing, please mark our initial in a diamond, under which comes the destination with the contract number. In addition, ③indicative marks such as HANDLE WITH CARE, DO NOT DROP, THIS SIDE UP should also be stenciled on both sides of the case.

④We are looking forward to your confirmation on the issue of packing.

Yours faithfully,

---

① With reference to the packing of our Order No. 135 for 1,000 cases of Australian wines

　a. _____

　b. _____

② we suggest that the Australian wines be packed in seaworthy cases capable of withstanding rough handling

　a. _____

　b. _____

③ indicative marks such as HANDLE WITH CARE, DO NOT DROP, THIS SIDE UP should also be stenciled on both sides of the case

　a. _____

　b. _____

④ We are looking forward to your confirmation on the issue of packing

　a. _____

　b. _____

Letter Writing

♣ Practice 6

Compose a letter of packing instruction with the given information.

① all the goods will be in good condition

② should be stenciled

③ be packed in international standard tea boxes

④ reads as follows

⑤ add our initials ABC in a diamond

⑥ we find that the packing clauses in it are not clear enough

Dear Sirs,

 We have received your letter dated 8 October, enclosing the above sales contract in duplicate. But after going through the contract, _____. The relative clauses _____:

 The black tea under the contract should _____, 24 boxes on a pallet, and 10 pallets in an FCL container. On the outer packing please _____, under which the port of destination and our order number should be marked. In addition, warning marks like KEEP DRY, USE NO HOOK _____.

 We feel sure that you will meet our requirements so as to ensure that _____ when reaching the destination.

 We look forward to receiving your shipping advice.

Yours faithfully,

♣ Practice 7

Write a letter of packing instruction according to the information given below.

★ 贵方 7 月 15 日第 579 号订单已收到，除包装条款外，其他条款我方都能接受。

★ 介绍我方雨衣产品的包装详情：先用塑料袋装好后放入纸盒内，8 打装 1 纸箱，每箱毛重约 15 公斤。每一纸箱内用塑料做衬，整个纸箱用铁箍加固，这样能避免货物因受潮或粗鲁搬运而造成损失。

★ 我方认为每件雨衣用塑料袋包装后看上去更美观，可在商店的橱窗陈列，也将有利于销售。另外，改进后的包装重量轻，易于搬运。

♣ Practice 8

Complete the letter according to the Chinese in the parentheses.

Dear Sirs,

 We have received the captioned contract in two copies yesterday. ① _____

 _____(经详阅，很遗憾告知合同中的包装条款不是很清楚). To avoid possible problems in the future, ② _____ (包装要求如下):

③_____ （每台机器应用木箱包装，10木箱为1集装箱）.

On the outer packing please add our initials CACS in a triangle, under which the port of destination and our order number should be stenciled. In addition, warning marks like "keep upright", "keep from moisture and water", should also be indicated.

④_____ （如贵方能早日确认我方的包装方案，我们将不胜感激）.

Yours faithfully,

Part Ⅳ Supplementary Reading

Reading One

Dear Sirs,

In reply to your letter of May 15 inquiring about the packing of our computer components, we indicate as follows:

Our computer components for export are packed in boxes of one dozen each, 200 boxes to a carton. Its dimension is 18cm high, 30cm wide and 60cm long with a volume of about 0.034 cubic meter. The gross weight is 26.5kg, and the net is 25.5kg. As to the shipping marks outside the carton, besides the gross, net weight and tare, the wording "MADE IN CHINA" is also stenciled on the package. If you have any additional preference in this respect, please let us know and we will do our utmost to meet your requirements.

Using this opportunity, we would like to inform you that we used to pack our computer components in wooden cases, but after several trial shipments in carton packing, we found our cartons just as seaworthy as wooden cases. In addition, cartons are less expensive, is lighter to carry and cost lower freight. Nowadays, more and more clients are preferring carton packing to wooden case packing. We believe that you will agree to our opinion and accept our carton packing.

We are looking forward to your favorable reply.

Yours faithfully,

Reading Two

Dear Sirs

We are pleased to advise you that the 400 dozen sweaters under Order No. 1366 packed in cartons were shipped on board S.S "Fengqing" on June 16 to be transshipped at Hong Kong. We shall appreciate it if you can inform us of the condition of packing as soon as the goods reach your end.

If the consignments above are packed in cartons, we wish to give you the benefits as follows:

★ Packing in cartons protects skilful pilferage. As the trace of pilferage will be more in evidence, the insurance company may be made to pay the necessary compensation for such losses.

★ Because cartons are comparatively light and compact, they are more convenient to handle in loading and unloading. Besides, the rate of breakage is lower than that of wooden cases in transport.

In consideration of the above-mentioned reasons, it is believed that your clients will find packing in cartons more satisfactory.

We are awaiting your further response.

Yours faithfully,

Lesson Thirteen ••●

Shipment

Objectives

To be proficient in

◎ understanding the main information and key terms often used in a letter of shipment

◎ writing a letter with information about shipment

Writing Tips

Shipment is the process of transporting commodities and cargo, by land, air, or sea. The letters of shipment usually involve information about the date and number of the contract, the date and number of bill of lading, the names of commodities and their quality and value, the name of the carrying vessel, the name of the shipping port/loading port, the estimated time of departure, the name of the destination port, the estimated time of arrival, and a list of the relevant shipping documents.

Part I
Warm-up Activities

◆ **Write out the common methods of shipment according to the following pictures.**

_____

_____

◆ **Give more modes of shipment after discussion with your partner.**

Part Ⅱ
Sample Study

Sample 1

May 14, 2011

Dear Sir or Madam,

Thank you for your *Purchase* Order No. 0918, dated April 28 for 5,000 girl's dresses.

We are glad to *inform* you your order have been shipped per S.S. "PENELOPE", which is *scheduled* to sail from Ningbo on May 14th and the *estimated* time of arrival at Los Angles is May 26th.

We believe the goods will reach you in good condition and give you entire satisfaction. We hope this order will be the beginning of a long-term business relationship between us.

We look forward to the next opportunity to be of *assistance*. Please don't *hesitate* to call upon us any time.

Yours sincerely,

Sample 2

May 27, 2011

Dear Sir or Madam,

Our Order No. 0918 for 5,000 Girl's Dresses

This is to *acknowledge* the receipt of the above referenced order and to inform you that there is an error in the *shipment*.

We ordered dresses in sizes 14 to 24, yet some of the dresses we received were in wrong size.

Upon receiving your *instructions* for the return of goods, we will send the incorrect *merchandise* back to you.

We would like to receive the correct merchandise as quickly as possible and will appreciate your *expeditious* handling of this matter.

Yours sincerely,

Vocabulary

purchase	/ˈpɜːtʃəs/	v. 购买
inform	/ɪnˈfɔːm/	v. 告诉，通知，通报，报告
schedule	/ˈskedʒʊl/	v. 排定，安排，把……列入计划
estimated	/ˈestəmeɪtɪd/	a. 估计的
assistance	/əˈsɪstəns/	n. 帮助，援助，支持
hesitate	/ˈhezəteɪt/	v. 犹豫；顾虑；疑虑
acknowledge	/əkˈnɒlɪdʒ/	v. 告知已收到，承认，供认
shipment	/ˈʃɪpmənt/	n. 船运；运输，装运
instruction	/ɪnˈstrʌkʃən/	n. 指示；用法
merchandise	/ˈmɜːtʃəndaɪz/	n. 商品，货物
expeditious	/ˌekspɪˈdɪʃəs/	a. 迅速有效的，快速完成的

Notes

1. inform 告诉，通知

I am sorry for failing to inform you immediately.

未能及时通知，我深表歉意。

Please inform him that his parcel reached me.

麻烦告诉他，我收到了他的包裹。

inform sb. of sth. 通知/告诉某人某事

Please inform us of the shipping date.

请通知我们装船的日期。

You should inform your client of the risks.

你应该告诉客户合同的风险所在。

inform by 通过……（方式）告诉，通知

inform by letter 函告

inform by telegraph 电告

2. schedule *v.* 排定，安排

The secretary is trying to schedule the month's appointments.

秘书正在设法安排这个月的约会。

schedule *n.* 时间表，日程安排表

The manager has a tight schedule this month.

这个月经理的日程安排很紧。

The goods we ordered have arrived on schedule.

我们所订的货物已如期运到。

3. acknowledge 告知已收到

acknowledge (the receipt of) a letter

表示收到来信

We must acknowledge his letter.

我们应该告诉他信收到了。

We acknowledge with thanks (the) receipt of your letter of May 28.

谢谢你方 5 月 28 日来信。

This is to acknowledge the receipt of your letter.

来函敬悉。

4. shipment 船运，水运，运输，运送，装运

time of shipment 装运期，装运时间

partial shipment 分批装运

prompt shipment 即期装运

port of shipment 装运港

term of shipment 装船条件

The shipment is ready, please expedite credit.

船已经装完，请速开信用证。

The shipment is expected to take 15 days.

装船预计需要 15 天。

We have reached an agreement with him in regard to the shipment.

我们已经就装运问题同他达成协议。

As requested, we will inform you of the date of dispatch immediately upon completing shipment.

按照你方要求，我们会在装运完成后立即将发货日期通知你方。

shipment *n.* (从海路、陆路或空运的) 一批货物；运输的货物

The shipment we received is short.

我们收到的货物数量短缺。

Our shipment can reach the destination before June 26.

货物于6月26日前到达目的地。

Expressions

For sending shipping advice

1. We are glad to inform you your order has been shipped per S.S. …, which is scheduled to sail from… on… and the estimated time of arrival at … is ….

2. We have the pleasure of informing you that the goods under Contract No. … have been shipped today by … (ship) from port A to port B.

3. The goods you ordered will be shipped below deck.

4. We are pleased to advise you that we have completed the shipment of your order…

For delivery time

1. I wonder if it is possible for you to effect shipment in June.

2. I'd like to know if there is any possibility of dispatching the goods by the end of June.

3. We expect that you are in a position to make shipment by the middle of June.

4. I wish to know if the goods can be sent in the early June.

For earlier shipment

1. We wonder if it is possible to advance the shipment.

2. We wish you would dispatch the goods as early as possible.

3. We're writing in the hope that you can offer an early shipment.

4. We hope you can ship the goods at an early date.

Part Ⅲ
Practical Writing

Main Information

♣ Practice 1

Complete the following chart according to Sample 1.

Order No.: _____

Goods: _____

Date of shipment: _____

The estimated time of arrival: _____

Key Phrases

♣ Practice 2

Translate the following phrases into Chinese or English.

English	Chinese
estimated time of departure	_____

shipping advice   _____

delivery date   _____

shipping documents   _____

bill of lading   _____

_____   到期，满期

_____   装运

_____   完整无损

_____   交货

_____   备妥待运

❖ Practice 3

Complete the following sentences with the proper form of the words or phrases given in the box.

dispatch	shipment	acknowledge	advise	delay
due	expedite	enclose	deadline	port

1. We _____ receipt of your letter dated June 2.

2. There must be no _____ in forwarding the goods.

3. We assure you that we shall do our utmost to _____ shipment.

4. Please _____ the goods we ordered by sea.

5. It cost us a lot of money to get the goods from the _____ to our factory.

6. Can you possibly effect _____ more promptly?

7. The ship was _____ to sail the following morning.

8. We shall _____ you when the shipment is made.

9. I _____ herewith two copies of the contract.

10. We had hoped for an extension of the _____ to the end of the week.

Useful Expressions

❖ Practice 4

Complete the following sentences in English.

1. We are glad to inform you that 货物已经装运 . (ship)

         运到的货情况良好 . (in good condition)

2. We will try our best to 尽早发货 . (as early as possible)

         满足你方的需求 . (meet)

3. We have the pleasure to 同函寄上提单 . (enclose)

         告知我方已提货 . (take delivery of the goods)

♣ Practice 5

Rewrite the underlined parts in the letter below with two different expressions, but without changing the meaning of the sentences.

July 26th, 2011

Dear Sirs,

①We are pleased to inform you that we have completed the shipment of your order No. 0312. The estimated time of departure is 10:18 a.m. today from Zhanjiang and ②the estimated time of arrival at Sydney is on the morning of August 4th.

This morning we have airmailed the following documents so that you may take delivery of the goods when they reach port:

◆ One original of signed commercial invoice

◆ Packing list in triplicate

◆ One non-negotiable copy of Bill of Lading

◆ One copy of Manufacturers' Certificate of Quality

③We trust the goods will reach you in good order and assure you that ④all your future orders will continue to receive our immediate and careful attention.

Yours faithfully,

① We are pleased to advise you that we have completed the shipment of your order No. 0312

a. _____

b. _____

② the estimated time of arrival at Sydney is on the morning of August 4th

a. _____

b. _____

③ We trust the goods will reach you in good condition

a. _____

b. _____

④ all your future orders will continue to receive our immediate and careful attention

a. _____

b. _____

Letter Writing

♣ Practice 6

Compose a letter urging shipment with the given information.

① the contracted time of delivery is rapidly falling due

② give us your prompt response without further delay

③ Any delay in shipping or booked orders will undoubtedly cause us trouble

④ We are writing to draw your attention to the fact

⑤ we made it clear that we were in an urgent situation

Sept. 1, 2011

Tom Williams

ABC Co. Ltd.

11 Edith Street,

Hackney West, London

Dear Sirs,

_____ that up to now we have not received from you any information about the order, while _____.

When the order was placed, _____. We have to deliver the goods to our customer before the deadline on Sept. 10. _____.

Please look into the matter and _____.

Yours faithfully,

Tony Montana

Practice 7

Write a reply to the letter of Practice 6 according to the information below.

You are Tom Williams, the sales manager of ABC Company. You received the letter from Tony Montana for urging shipment. Now you are writing back to apologize for the delay in shipment, and tell him that it's because of an unexpectedly large volume of orders this season, but you can arrange the order to be delivered on Sept. 3 and the estimated time of arrival is on Sept. 12.

Practice 8

Complete the following letter according to the Chinese in the parentheses.

March 29, 2011

Dear Sirs,

This is to inform you that ①_____ (我方无法按规定日期发货).

We should have our merchandise ②_____ (交货日期前十五天准备发货) and we hope that you can hold off until that time.

We can assure you that if your order remains in force we will expedite delivery to you as soon as we have received the merchandise.

③_____ (对此次延误我们深表歉意) and thank you for your understanding.

Yours sincerely,

Part Ⅳ Supplementary Reading

Reading One

Dear Sirs,

Thank you for your extension of your L/C No. 2346. Today we shipped the consignment by the direct steamer "Ocean Queen" which sails for your port tomorrow.

Enclosed please find one set of the shipping documents covering this consignment, which comprises the commercial invoice, bill of lading, packing list, certificate of origin and insurance certificate.

We are pleased to have filled your order after long delay and trust that the goods will reach you in good order to meet your urgent requirement and that they will turn out to your complete satisfaction.

We will receive your future orders promptly and carefully.

Yours sincerely,

Reading Two

Dear Sirs,

Referring to our letters in respect to Order No. 5241 for six cases of silk handkerchiefs, so far we have no definite information from you about delivery time, although these goods are stipulated for shipment before the end of last month, and our L/C was opened with the Bank of China as early as in March 2011.

We have been put to considerable inconvenience by the delay in delivery. You should inform us immediately of the earliest possible date of shipment. If you can't effect delivery within the stipulated time, we will have to lodge a claim against you for the loss and reserve the right to cancel the contract.

Please look up the matter and give us your definite reply without further delay.

Yours faithfully,

Lesson Fourteen •●●

Insurance

Objectives

To be proficient in

◎ understanding the main information and key terms often used in a letter of insurance

◎ writing a letter of insurance

Writing Tips

Insurance is a way to protect the buyer or the seller against the financial loss which he would otherwise suffer in case damage or loss of goods was inflicted upon him in the course of transportation. The letter of insurance generally contains information about inquiring about insurance information, asking the seller to cover insurance, discussing insurance clause, etc.

Part I
Warm-up Activities

◆ Write out the full names of the insurance companies shown below.

◆ **Give more names of insurance companies after discussion with your partner.**

Part II
Sample Study

Sample 1

December 5, 2011

Dear Sir or Madam,

We have a *consignment* of 4,000 sets of *light fixtures* to be shipped from Tianjin China to Sydney, valued at US $ 800,000.

We wish to have this consignment *insured* by your company against *All Risks*. The insurance is going from the port of Tianjin to Sydney. Therefore we are writing to enquire about the terms and conditions which you can provide.

We would appreciate your sending us your present insurance policy at your earliest convenience.

Yours sincerely,

Sample 2

December 6, 2011

Dear Sir or Madam,

In reply to your letter dated December 5, enquiring about the insurance information, we would like to inform you of the following:

All Risks will cover losses from all causes occurring at any time throughout the whole currency of the *coverage*, *irrespective of*

whether they are caused by accidents at sea or on land. If you wish to cover All Risks, our rate for your goods is 120% of the *declared* value.

We trust the above information will meet your requirements and hope to hear from you soon.

Yours sincerely,

Vocabulary

consignment	/kən'saɪnmənt/	*n.* 托付货物，托卖货物
insure	/ɪn'ʃʊə/	*v.* 投保；承保
coverage	/'kʌvərɪdʒ/	*n.* 覆盖范围（或方式）
declare	/dɪ'kleə/	*v.* 宣布，宣告，申报
light fixture		电灯组件，电灯器具
All Risks		一切险
irrespective of		不受……的影响；不管

Notes

1. insure

Please insure us on the following goods against All Risks.

请将我方以下货物投保一切险。

Please insure F.P.A. at your end.

请在你处投保平安险。

We have insured the shipment W.P.A.

我们已为货物投保水渍险。

Generally speaking, we insure W.P.A on CIF sales.

一般来讲，如果是以 CIF 价成交的话，我们投保水渍险。

Please insure us on the following goods.

请为我们投保下列货物。

2. coverage

insurance coverage　保险范围

This is an insurance policy with extensive coverage.

这是一项承保范围广泛的保险。

Please give us the policy rates for F.P.A. coverage.

请给我方平安险的保险费率。

The coverage is W.P.A. plus Risk of Breakage.

投保的险别为水渍险加破碎险。

3. types of insurance

primary types of insurance: F.P.A ; W.P.A; AR 基本险

F.P.A (Free from Particular Average) 平安险

WA /W.P.A (With Particular Average) 水渍险

AR (All Risks) 一切险

General Additional Risk 一般附加险

TPND (THEFT, PILFERAGE AND NON-DELIVERY) 偷窃提货不着险

FWRD (Fresh Water and/or Rain Damage) 淡水雨淋险

Leakage Risk 渗漏险

Shortage Risk 短量险

Intermixture & Contamination 混杂和玷污险 / 霉变

Clash and Breakage Risk 碰损、破碎险

Taint of Odour Risk 串味险

Sweat and Heating Risk 受潮受热险

Hook Damage Risk 钩损险

Breakage of Packing Risk 包装破裂险

Rust Risk 锈损险

Special Additional Risk 特别附加险

Failure to Deliver 交货不到险

Contingent Import Duty 进口关税险

On Deck Risk 舱面货物险

Rejection Risk 拒收险

Aflatoxin Risk 黄曲霉素险

FREC (Fire Risk Extention Clause for Storage of Cargo of Destination Hongkong Including Kowloon, or Macao) 出口货物到香港或澳门存仓火险责任扩展条款

War Risk 战争险

SRCC (insurance against strike, riot and civil commotion) 罢工险

Expressions

For asking for insurance

1. I am looking for insurance from your company and I want to know what types of cover you usually underwrite.

2. We wish to cover insurance on the goods against…risk for 110% of invoice value with the insurer.

3. We are willing to take out FPA and WPA covers for the shipment.

4. We would like to know whether you can undertake insurance on wine against All Risks.

For replying the insurance request

1. We have the pleasure of informing you that we have insured your Order No. ...for the invoice cost plus 20% up to the port of destination.

2. We would like to inform you that we have covered the shipment against All Risks for US $ 8,300 with the People's Insurance Company of China.

3. We agree to your request to insure the shipment for 130% of the invoice value, but the premium for the difference between 130% and 110% should be for your account.

4. We can cover the inland insurance on your behalf, but you will have to pay an additional premium.

For expectation of reply

1. We sincerely hope that our request will meet with your approval.

2. We are awaiting your early reply.

3. We would be grateful if you could handle this business quickly.

4. We hope the above will be acceptable to you.

Part III
Practical Writing

Main Information

♣ Practice 1

Complete the following chart according to Sample 1.

Consignment: _____

The commencement to termination of insurance: _____

Insurance to cover: _____

Writing purpose: _____

Key Phrases

♣ Practice 2

Translate the following phrases into Chinese or English.

English	Chinese
overland transportation insurance	_____
general additional risks	_____
Actual Total Loss	_____
with particular average (W.P.A.)	_____

free from particular average (F.P.A.) _____

_____ 保险单

_____ 保险费

_____ 保险条款

_____ 保险索赔

_____ 保险

Practice 3

Complete the following sentences with the proper form of the words or phrases given in the box below.

effect	insure	in the absence of	delete	in regard to
cover	franchise	for the buyer's account	claim	consign

1. Please _____ the goods against ocean marine cargo insurance.

2. Insurance of the goods is to be _____ by us for 110% of the CIF value.

3. As a rule, the extra premium involved will be _____.

4. Please _____ the words "insurance certificate or policy" from the L/C.

5. We usually cover insurance against All Risks _____ the buyers' detailed requirements.

6. What kind of insurance are you able to provide for my _____?

7. _____ are payable only for that part of the loss, that is over 8%.

8. We have received your letter _____ insurance.

9. Please _____ insurance on your side.

10. The class of merchandise is sold with a _____ of 4%.

Useful Expressions

Practice 4

Complete the following sentences in English.

1. We shall be pleased if you will arrange to 将此货投保一切险 . (insure…against)

　　　　　　　　　　　　　　　 投保水渍险和战争险 . (war risk)

2. We shall 代表贵方安排保险 . (arrange… on one's behalf)

　　　会提供保险但费用由你负担 . (at one's cost)

　　　自己投保 . (cover)

3. We'd like to 按超过发票金额的 10% 部分投保 . (invoice value)

　　　　按发票金额的 110% 投保 . (effect)

Practice 5

Rewrite the underlined parts in the letter below with two different expressions, but without changing the meaning of the sentences.

May 13, 2011

Dear Sirs,

①This is to acknowledge receipt of your letter dated May 12, requiring us to insure the captioned shipment for an amount of 20% above the invoice value.

We are glad to inform you that ②we have insured the above shipment against All Risks for US $ 8,300 with the People's Insurance Company of China. Although our usual practice is to ③insure the goods for 10% above invoice value, we are prepared to comply with your request for getting cover for 120% of the invoice value. But ④you should pay for the additional premium.

We are looking forward to your prompt response.

Yours faithfully,

① This is to acknowledge receipt of your letter dated May 12

a. _____

b. _____

② We have insured the above shipment against All Risks

a. _____

b. _____

③ insure the goods for 10% above invoice value

a. _____

b. _____

④ you should pay for the additional premium

a. _____

b. _____

Letter Writing

Practice 6

Compose a letter asking the seller to cover insurance with the given information.

① if you can kindly arrange to insure the same on our behalf against All Risks

② our request will meet with your approval

③ you may draw on us at sight for the same

④ which was placed on CFR basis

⑤ We shall refund the premium to you upon receipt of your debit note

June 12, 2011

Dear Sirs,

　　We wish to refer you to our order No. 1001 for 500 bicycles, _____.

　　As we would like you to effect insurance on your side, we shall be pleased _____

_____ at invoice value plus 10%.

　　_____ or, if you like, _____.

　　We sincerely hope that _____.

Yours faithfully,

♣ Practice 7

Write a letter requiring the seller to insure according to the information below.

　　Recently you ordered 200 cases of toys under Sales Contract No. 1408. Now you are writing a letter to request the seller to cover insurance for 120% of the invoice value against All Risks. As the seller only insures the shipments for 10% above the invoice value, you can pay for the extra premium for additional coverage. Now write a letter to them, hoping to handle this business quickly.

♣ Practice 8

Complete the reply to the letter of Practice 7 according to the Chinese in the parentheses.

August 24, 2011

Dear Sirs,

　　Thank you for your letter dated August 21, requesting us to ①_____ (代办标题货物的保险) for your account.

　　We are pleased to inform you that ②_____ (我们已为上述货物投保) with The People's Insurance Company of China against All Risks for USD4,000. If coverage against other additional risks is demanded, the entire premium thus arising from it will be borne by you.

　　③_____ (我们正在开列保险单) accordingly and will be forwarded to you by the end of this month together with our ④_____ (保险费的索款通知单).

Yours sincerely,

Manager

Part IV
Supplementary Reading

Reading One

Dear Sirs,

Referring to S/C No. 146 covering 1,000 tons of cotton, we would like to inform you that we have issued with the Bank of China a confirmed, irrevocable L/C No. 278 amounting to $1,200,000 with validity until 21st May.

Please note that the goods mentioned must be dispatched before the end of April and insured against All Risks for 120% of the invoice value. We know your usual practice is to insure the goods only for full invoice value. Therefore, the extra premium will be for our account.

Please send us your shipping advice as soon as possible.

Yours sincerely,

Reading Two

April 26th, 2011

Dear Sirs,

This is to acknowledge receipt of your letter dated April 25th, inquiring about the insurance on the above-mentioned order.

For the goods on CIF basis, we will insure against All Risks and War Risk for 100% of the invoice value. If you demand to cover against other additional risks, the extra premium involved will be for buyer's account. The insurance shall terminate, when the goods are delivered to the consignee's warehouse at the destination named in the policy. It should be noted that the coverage is limited to 60 days upon discharge of the insured goods from seagoing vessel at the final port of discharge before the insured goods reach the consignee's warehouse.

If any damage to the goods occurs, a claim may be filed with the insurance agent of PICC at your end, who will undertake to compensate you for the loss sustained. The principal perils which the basic marine policy of the PICC insures against under its Ocean Marine Cargo Clauses are: FPA, WPA and All Risks.

Please contact the PICC on your side for further particulars.

Unit 6

Complaint and Claim

Complaints

Objectives

To be proficient in

◎ understanding the main information and key terms often used in a complaint letter

◎ writing a letter of complaint

Writing Tips

During the process of a contract execution in international trade, if one party fails to perform the contract properly, the other party who suffers damages or losses has the right to complain according to the relevant terms of the contract.

Here are some guidelines:

● the tone should be polite and friendly;

● the letter should be based on maintaining the original trade relationship between the two parties;

● the offered information should be true and credible.

Part I
Warm-up Activities

◆ Discuss in groups and write out some reasons which may result in complaints as possible as you can.

◆ Work in groups and discuss the question.

How to deal with complaints?

Part II
Sample Study

Sample 1

November 20, 2011

Overseas Economic Trading Company

112-15 Daogu-Dong, Seoul, Korea

Dear Sir or Madam,

Our Order No. 234 for *stationery* has duly arrived and we have taken *delivery* of the goods. Upon careful examination, to our great disappointment, the goods do not *match* the samples you sent us, and the quality of the goods is not up to our expectations. In fact, the quality is so poor that it's impossible to meet the *requirements* of our clients.

Therefore, we are *obliged* to return the delivered goods and require a replacement for the quantity ordered fully. We hope you will *do your utmost to rectify* this situation. If you can replace the goods, we are prepared to extend the delivery date to December 22. We hope to receive your reply no later than December 5.

We look forward to your prompt response.

Yours sincerely,

Sample 2

December 10, 2011

Wenyang Import and Export Corp.

25 Huangxing Road, Changsha

P.R.China

Dear Sir/Madam,

In reference to your letter of November 20, we are sorry for the poor quality of the stationery products supplied to Order No. 234. We have brought your complaint to our prompt attention.

We have *investigated* the matter and found out that the goods do not conform to the samples. The survey report indicates that it resulted from mechanical *malfunctions* which *subsequently* influenced the quality of the products.

We are arranging for the correct goods to be dispatched to you. The relevant documents will also be mailed to you as soon as possible. It is appreciated if you can accept our apology for the trouble and inconvenience we caused you.

Yours sincerely,

Vocabulary

complaint	/kəmˈpleɪnt/	*n.* 抱怨；诉苦
stationery	/ˈsteɪʃənərɪ/	*n.* 文具
delivery	/dɪˈlɪvərɪ/	*n.* 传送，运送，交付的东西
match	/mætʃ/	*v.* 和……一致，和……相配
requirement	/rɪˈkwaɪəmənt/	*n.* 必需品；要求
oblige	/əˈblaɪdʒ/	*v.* 使非做……不可；迫使……做某事
rectify	/ˈrektɪˌfaɪ/	*v.* 改正；更正
investigate	/ɪnˈvestɪgeɪt/	*v.* 调查；检查；研究
malfunction	/mælˈfʌŋkʃən/	*n.* 故障；功能障碍
subsequently	/ˈsʌbsɪkwəntlɪ/	*adv.* (作为后果) 随后地

| do one's utmost | 尽最大努力 |
| in reference to | 关于 |

Notes

1. complaint

make/lodge a complaint against/about…to sb. …

就……向……投诉

There's been a number of complaints about the standard of service.

已有对服务水准的大量投诉。

The buyer made a complaint against the poor quality of the machines to the supplier.

买主就机器的低劣质量向供应商投诉。

2. match: be exactly like; correspond exactly

This shipment didn't match the sample you showed us last month.

这批货与上个月你给我们看的样品不符。

64 percent said their salary rises could not match the economic development.

64% 的人认为他们的工资涨幅与经济发展不相称。

The price of this commodity does not match its value at all.

这件商品的价钱与它的价值很不相称。

3. be obliged to 使非做……不可，迫使……做某事

oblige: to make it necessary for sb. to do sth.

Falling profits obliged them to close the factory.

利润下降迫使他们关闭这家工厂。

I was obliged to leave after such an unpleasant business negotiation.

因为这次不愉快的商务谈判，我必须离开。

4. do one's utmost to

utmost: the most that can be done

I did my utmost to trace the delivery process to ensure the delivery on time.

我尽最大努力跟踪发货进程以确保准时发货。

The seller tries his utmost to meet the clients requirements.

5. in reference to: in connection with; about

In reference to your recent letter, I was sorry about your complaint.

关于你最近的来信，我对你们的投诉非常抱歉。

In reference to our representative's call, we've learned that we have obtained the receipt for the goods.

通过查询我方代表电话，我们得知已收到货物收据。

In reference to your offer of October 1st, we have no interest in these goods because the quantities are too small.

鉴于贵方 10 月 1 日的发盘，因为数量太少，我方尚无兴趣。

6. investigate : look into; inquire into; go into; make an investigation into

After investigating the matter, we found out that the damage was caused by mishandling at the dock.

经调查，我们发现损坏是由码头作业不小心引起的。

The manager decided to investigate the affair.

经理决定对此事进行调查。

7. conform

conform to/with 符合；与……一致

Do these designs conform to the official specifications of the shipment?

这些设计图是否符合装运的正式规格？

It will ensure that all communication conforms to your security policy.

它可以保证所有的通信符合安全政策。

You will be responsible for the shortages, defects or anything which don't conform with the contract.

货物有短少、缺陷或任何与合同规定不符的情况，将由你方负责赔偿。

in conformity with 与……一致

conformity: agreement with established rules, customs, etc.

We regret to tell you that the goods specifications you sent us are not in conformity with that stipulated in the contract.

很遗憾，你方运来的货物规格与合同不符。

Please check all the terms in the contract and see if there is anything not in conformity with the terms we agreed on.

请您逐项检查合同的所有条款，看是否有与我们达成的协议有不符之处。

 Expressions

When making a complaint

1. I am writing to complain about…

2. We have to protest about the late delivery of…

3. We regret to report that some of the goods are badly damaged…

4. To our disappointment, the goods do not match the samples…

For requesting

1. We hope you will do your utmost to rectify the situation.

2. We have no choice but to ask for a replacement.

3. We need to put in a claim for damage.

4. We are obliged to return the goods…

For accepting complaint

1. We are deeply concerned about the complaint about…

2. Thank you for reporting this matter, since…

3. With reference to your letter of…, we are sorry that…

4. We are sorry to learn from your letter of…

For expressing an apology

1. We apologize once more for the mistake.

2. We ask you to accept our apologies for the trouble and inconvenience we have caused you.

3. We'd like to apologize for this incident.

4. We wish to express our deep regret at this case.

Part III
Practical Writing

Main Information

♣ Practice 1

Complete the following chart according to Sample 1.

Object of complaint: _____

Intention: _____

Reason: _____

Requirements: _____

Key Phrases

♣ Practice 2

Translate the following phrases into Chinese or English.

English	Chinese
_____	提货
_____	令人遗憾／失望
_____	与样品相符
_____	与样品不一致
_____	投诉
replacement of the quantity ordered	_____
return the shipment	
a shortage in the shipment	
badly damaged	
short (in) weight by	

♣ Practice 3

Complete the following sentences with the proper form of the words or phrases given in the box below.

match	make	complain about	look into	inform
agree to	take delivery of	have no choice but	resulted from	replace

1. Great losses arose from rough handling, so compensation should _____ by the shipper.

2. We should _____ those damaged goods during the shipment.

3. The receiver has the right to _____ the wrong delivery.

4. When the agent is _____ of the situation, he will take it into consideration.

5. The materials do not _____ the samples you sent us.

6. We _____ to return them to you and require a replacement.

7. Do you think he will _____ my suggestion?

8. The damage to the goods _____ the porter's carelessness.

9. We _____ the goods which arrived at the port.

10. After _____ the matter, we find the wrong delivery was caused by mishandling.

♣ Practice 4

Complete the following sentences in English.

1. We regret to report that 部分货物已严重受损. (badly damaged)
   货物与样品不一致. (differ from)

2. To our disappointment, 产品质量未达到我方要求. (up to)
   我们失去了一个极佳的促销时机. (lose)

3. We apologize for 因此次错误发货给贵方造成的不便. (cause)
   延迟提交7月2号订购的货物. (late delivery)

♣ Practice 5

Rewrite the underlined parts in the letter below with two different expressions, but without changing the meaning of the sentences.

July 6, 2011

Dear Sir or Madam,

①Much to my regret, we have to place a complaint about the bad delivery service in your company.

The Samsung Tape Recorders Model No. JB/4073 which we ordered on July 1 arrived yesterday. ②We are sorry to report that some recorders have been badly damaged. When we opened them, we found that some lids had been cracked.

Since there was damage to the goods, we have decided to file a complaint against the delivery service. ③<u>We're obliged to return the damaged recorders to you</u>. We are grateful if you can replace them as soon as possible.

Looking forward to your early reply.

Sincerely yours,

Jonathan Edwards

Manager

① Much to my regret, we have to place a complaint about the bad delivery service in your company

a. _____

b. _____

② We are sorry to report that some recorders have been badly damaged

a. _____

b. _____

③ We 're obliged to return the damaged recorders to you

a. _____

b. _____

Letter Writing

♣ **Practice 6**

Compose a complaint letter with the given information.

① Wuhan Import and Export Corp. of China

② you can supply the correct materials

③ we have taken delivery of the goods

④ the quality of the materials was not up to expectation

⑤ to require a replacement of the quantity ordered

⑥ If you are kind to replace the materials

October 22, 2011

_____

239 Dufudi Road, Wuchang

Wuhan 430061

P.R.China

Dear Sir or Madam,

Our order of 6 May for upholstery materials has duly arrived and _____.

After examining the shipment carefully, much to our regret, _____.

Your goods cannot be accepted because they differ from the samples and are unsuited to the needs of our products.

We have no choice but to return them to you and _____. We hope you will do your utmost to rectify this situation. _____, and forward the right order, we are prepared to allow the agreed delivery time to run from the date when _____.

We look forward to your early reply.

Yours faithfully,

Park Junshou

♣ Practice 7

Write a complaint letter according to the information given below.

说明：假设你是步步高百货公司采购部的经理 John Smith, 请以公司的名义向东方电子公司写一封投诉信。

投诉商品：MD300 手机（12 月 19 日购买）

投诉原因：不能拍照，不能收发短信，自动关机等等

投诉要求：退货或更换

提出希望：尽快处理

写信日期：2011 年 12 月 21 日

♣ Practice 8

Complete the reply to the letter of Practice 7 according to the Chinese in the parentheses.

December 22, 2011

Dear Sir,

We have received your letter of Dec 21st. I'm sorry for the problems of the cell phones. ①_____ (基于我们公司售后服务的政策), we are currently reviewing your complaints and suggestions, and I assure you that we will make a careful study of them and ②_____ (尽快答复你所提的问题). We will replace the broken cell phones and ③_____ (希望继续信任我们).

Yours sincerely,

Li Gang

Part IV
Supplementary Reading

Reading One

Dear Sir or Madam,

We found there are many errors in the packages of PO:002 & PO:011.

PO:002: You packed 20 PCS in a carton without an inner box instead of 5 PCS/inner box & 4 inner box/carton as we ordered.

PO:011: 2,000 sets of DVD-I instead of DVD-II.

We are sorry that there is little demand for the goods that you have sent us due to the economic crisis. Therefore, we would be grateful if you would arrange for their collection and send us those we ordered as soon as possible. As we are a regular client, we hope that you will take urgent action to remedy the situation.

Look forward to your early reply.

Yours faithfully,

Reading Two

Dear Sirs,

We were glad to know that the consignment reached you within the stipulated time, but it was with much regret that we learned that there was a difference of 25 tons between the actual loaded weight and the invoiced weight.

This incident has had our immediate attention. We have looked into it closely. A careful investigation shows that the goods were well-packed before shipment and no shortage were found at that time. Maybe the short-weight you made a claim for happened in the course of transit. Therefore, it is advisable that you lodge a claim against the carrier or the insurance company, for our business was based on FOB. We don't think the responsibility should rest with us.

We hope that our proposal will be acceptable to you. We are looking forward to the early settlement of this matter.

Yours sincerely,

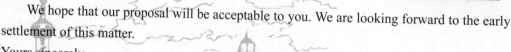

Claims

Objectives

To be proficient in

◎ understanding the main information and key terms often used in a claim letter

◎ writing a claim letter

Writing Tips

During the execution of a contract or the making of a transaction, if one party's behavior causes the loss of the other party, the party who suffers the loss reserves the right to lodge a claim against the other party, which has the obligation to solve the matter properly.

Here are some guidelines:

● the reply should be polite and sincere;

● the two parties should deal with the complaints on the basis of maintaining the original trade relationship;

● the offered information should be credible and the requirements should be reasonable.

Part I
Warm-up Activities

◆ **Work in groups and discuss the following question.**

> What should be included when you lodge a claim?

_____

_____

_____

◆ **Discuss in groups and tell whom you may make a claim to.**

> Whom may you make a claim to?

_____

_____

Part II
Sample Study

Sample 1

May 4, 2011

Dear Sir or Madam,

CONTRACT NO. 234 FOR <u>THE PURCHASE OF 30 METRIC TONS OF CHEMICAL FERTILIZER</u>

We *informed* you that the consignment arrived on 26 April. After *inspection,* we regret to note that 20 bags had burst and we have subsequently made a complete *inventory* of the broken items, estimated at 800kg, having been lost.

We have made a survey and the *survey report* confirmed our *initial findings*. It indicates that the loss was caused by the use of substandard bags which you should be *responsible* for.

In accordance with the contract, we intend to *lodge a claim* against you for the amount of GB £ 230.

Enclosed please find our Survey Report No.1234 and we look forward to an early settlement of the claim.

Yours sincerely,

Sample 2

Dear Sirs or Madam,

Thank you for your letter of the 4th of May. We are very sorry for the *short delivery* of 800kg chemical fertilizer due to the broken bags.

After investigating the matter, we have *ascertained* that the error was made by our warehouse staff and have discovered that they used the wrong bags for packing due to carelessness. The error is entirely our own and we apologize again for the inconvenience it has caused you.

We *are concerned with* maintaining our long-standing trade relationship, we thereby accept your claim and are sending you a check for GB £ 230 as compensation.

It is our sincere hope that this matter will not affect our future business relationship.

Yours sincerely,

Vocabulary

inform	/ɪnˈfɔːm/	v. 通知，告知
inspection	/ɪnˈspekʃən/	n. 检验；视察
inventory	/ˈɪnvənˌtɒrɪ/	n. 清单，详细目录
responsible	/rɪˈspɒnsəbl/	a. 负责的；有责任感的
ascertain	/ˌæsəˈteɪn/	v. 弄清，查明；确定
survey report		检验报告
initial finding		最初检验结果
lodge a claim		索赔
short delivery		短交，交货缺少
be concerned with		关注；重视

Notes

1. inform

inform sb. of/about sth.

I wasn't informed of the general manager's decision until it was too late.

等我得知总经理决定的时候，已经太迟了。

inform sb. that

I informed him that I would be unable to attend the meeting.

我通知他我不能出席会议。

Could you inform me on how to contact the company?

你能告诉我怎样与公司联络吗？

2. be responsible for 负责，承担责任

Who should be responsible for this terrible loss?

谁应为这一重大损失负责？

The manager has made me responsible for keeping the company in order while he went out.

经理外出时要我维持公司的秩序。

3. claim   *n.* 要求，索赔

lodge/make a claim on/for

When her house was burgled, she made a claim against the insurance company.

她的住宅失窃后，她向保险公司提出索赔。

claim   *v.* 索取，认领

claim on/for

Did you claim on the opposite company for the loss?

你有没有为那损失向对方公司索取赔偿？

4. ascertain   *v.* 弄清，确定，查明

They are doing everything possible to ascertain the reason for the late delivery.

他们正在尽力调查没有按时发货的原因。

Consumer surveys are designed to help ascertain whether or not a product will be successful on the market.

消费者调查表的设计有助于确定一件产品在市场上成功与否。

5. be concerned with/in doing 关注

be concerned to do 关注

The company is most concerned in the problem.

公司十分关注这个问题。

The dollar weakness is something to be concerned about.

美元的疲软确实值得担忧。

A successful investor should be concerned to operate successfully to achieve success.

一个成功的投资者应关注如何成功运作，以实现事业成功。

Industry sources are especially concerned about the steel price dropping again after the Chinese New Year.

工业企业十分关心中国新年之后钢材价格是否会再次下降。

 Expressions

For the reason of a claim

1. The quality of… was not up to our expectations, …

2. Upon examination, we found you have sent us the wrong goods.

3. Because of your late delivery, we lost a wonderful sales opportunity.

4. There is a shortage in the shipment of…

For claiming

1. We put in a claim for the damage / inferior quality.

2. We hereby bring up / make / raise /lodge a formal claim with you for the sum of… in all.

3. We cannot help lodging a claim against you for the amount of …

4. We need to have…either repaired or replaced.

For accepting a claim

1. We regret for the losses you have suffered and agree to compensate you for/to the sum/ amount …

2. We are prepared to compensate you for 10% of the total invoice value.

3. In view of our friendly relations, we agree to accept your full claim.

4. We agree to pay…for the mentioned quantity.

For rejecting a claim

1. We are sorry that we cannot accept responsibility for this claim.

2. We found no grounds to compensate for …

3. The evidence provided by you is insufficient, so we can't process your claim.

4. We regret that we are in no way responsible for the loss.

Part III
Practical Writing

Main Information

♣ Practice 1

Complete the following chart according to Sample 1.

Object of claim: _____

The intention: _____

Reason: _____

Requirements: _____

Key Phrases

♣ Practice 2

Translate the following phrases into Chinese or English.

English	Chinese
commodity inspection	_____
survey report	_____
claim settlement	_____
short delivery	_____
initial finding	_____
_____	与……进行核对
_____	对……负责
_____	凭借，根据
_____	索赔
_____	接受索赔

♣ Practice 3

Complete the following sentences with the proper form of the words or phrases given in the box below.

on the strength of	deliver	check	responsible	affect
in good condition	refer to	proceed	settle	shortage

1. _____ the survey report, we register our claim against £ 132.

2. We are not _____ for the damage because of the recipient's own carelessness.

3. We _____ Sales Contract No. 564 covering the purchase of 200 tons of cement.

4. As the case is _____, it's difficult for us to accept the claim.

5. We hope this unfortunate error will not _____ our future relationship.

6. We have _____ the complete inventory of the broken items.

7. We cannot help lodging a claim against you for late _____.

8. We are looking forward to _____ the claim as soon as possible.

9. The project is _____ according to the plan.

10. We find the case shows _____ in weight.

Useful Expressions

♣ Practice 4

Complete the following sentences in English.

1. On the strength of the survey report, 我们同意接受你方的全部索赔. (accept a claim)

   我们向贵方索赔150美元. (register claim)

2. A shortage of materials 导致我们无法接受新订单. (result in)

   导致我们巨大的损失. (cause)

3. Upon arrival of the shipment at our port, 我们立即重新检验了货物. (reinspect)

   我们发现货物远达不到标. (below the standard)

4. I suggest 贵方就赔偿问题与保险公司联系. (contact)

   你方尽早澄清和解决此事. (shortly)

♣ Practice 5

Rewrite the underlined parts in the letter below with two different expressions, but without changing the meaning of the sentences.

Dear Sirs,

We are surprised to learn from your letter of December 30 that the green beans dispatched on November 4 ①were below the standard as stipulated in the contract and that ②you are reserving the right to lodge a claim against us.

Naturally, we hope that the transaction will be concluded satisfactorily. Now that you have found ③the quality of the beans does not comply with that was stipulated in the contract, ④we want to have the problem clarified without delay. So, we have sent our representative to your end to conduct a detailed investigation. We shall not give any comments before our representative inspects the goods. We will let you know soon the date when he will visit. It is highly appreciated if you will give him your cooperation.

You may be assured that the matter will be settled in a reasonable manner to our mutual benefit.

Yours faithfully,

① were below the standard as stipulated in the contract

a. _____

b. _____

② you are reserving the right to lodge a claim against us

a. _____

b. _____

③ the quality of the beans does not comply with that was stipulated in the contract

a. _____

b. _____

④ we want to have the problem clarified without delay

a. _____

b. _____

Letter Writing

♣ Practice 6

Compose a claim letter with the information given below.

① the loss was due to careless handling

② covering the purchase of 2,000 glass products

③ we have hereby made a complete inventory of the damaged items

④ we regret to inform you that one of the cases was badly smashed

⑤ We look forward to your early settlement of the claim

Dear Sir or Madam,

We refer to Sales Contract No. 123 _____.

We emailed you that the consignment arrived on 15 May. Upon examination, _____

_____, the contents were seriously damaged and some glass products had been broken. We found out that about 100 pieces had irretrievably lost.

We have proceeded to conduct a report. The report indicates that _____ of the glass products by the warehouse staff from your company, therefore, you should be responsible for it.

On the strength of the survey report, _____ and register our claim against you for $15,000.

_____.

Yours faithfully,

♣ Practice 7

Write a letter of claim according to the information given below.

根据 No. 234 发货清单，贵方购买了 2 000 公斤优质大米，但 3 月 23 日货到后经检验发现短重 100 公斤，于是附寄调查报告，并向对方索赔 500 美元。

♣ Practice 8

Complete the reply to the letter of Practice 7 according to the Chinese in the parentheses.

Dear Sirs,

① _____ (非常感谢贵方3月24日的来信) and note with surprise that the polished rice shipped as per our Invoice No. 234 of February 25 ② _____

(短缺100公斤), which ③＿＿＿＿＿＿＿＿＿＿ (是由于仓库职员的粗心引起的). We therefore accept your claim and ④＿＿＿＿＿＿＿＿＿ (附上一张500美元的支票以解决此事). Please advise us of your receipt by email.

We hope you will accept our apologies and continue to entrust us with your orders.

Yours sincerely,

John Smith

Export Manager

Encl: Check No. 564 of US $500

Part Ⅳ Supplementary Reading

Reading One

Dear Sirs,

We are very surprised to learn from your letter of December 5 that the electronic fittings dispatched on November 4 were below the standard stipulated in the contract and that you are reserving the right to lodge a claim against us.

Naturally we hope that the transaction will be concluded to your satisfaction. Now that you have found the quality of the electronic fittings do not comply with that stipulated in the contract, we want to have the problem clarified without any delay. So we have sent our representative to your end to investigate the matter in detail. We shall not give any comments before our representative inspects the goods. Your best cooperation will be highly appreciated.

You may be assured that the matter will be settled in a reasonable manner to our mutual benefit.

Yours faithfully,

Reading Two

20 January, 2011

Dear Sir or Madam,

Thank you for your letter dated January 20. We are disappointed to hear that our price for Flame cigarette lighters is too high for you to accept. You have mentioned that Japanese goods are being offered to you at a price approximately 10% lower than that quoted by us.

We accept what you say, but we are of the opinion that the quality of the lighter do not measure up to that of our own.

Although we are keen to do business with you, we regret that we cannot accept your counter offer or even meet you half way. The best we can do is to reduce our previous quotation by 2%. We trust that this meets with your approval. We look forward to hearing from you.

Yours faithfully,

Tony Smith

Chief Seller

主要参考书目

[1] 晨梅梅.《实用写作教程》[M].上海：上海外语教育出版社，2006.

[2] 方春祥.《外贸函电》[M].北京：中国人民大学出版社，2005.

[3] 甘鸿.《外经贸英语函电》[M].上海：上海科学技术文献出版社，2004.

[4] 刘杰英.《世纪商务英语函电与单证》[M].大连：大连理工大学出版社，2007.

[5] 秦亚农等主编.《国际商贸英语函电教程》[M].长沙：中南大学出版社，2005.

[6] 齐智英.《商务外贸函电》[M].北京：机械工业出版社，2009.

[7] 全国外贸中等专业学校教材编写组.《对外经贸英语函电》[M].北京：对外经济贸易大学出版社，2003.

[8] 粟景妆.《商务外贸函电》[M].北京：冶金工业出版社，2009.

[9] 王虹、耿伟等主编.《外贸英语函电》[M].北京：清华大学出版社，2009.

[10] 王乃彦.《对外经贸英语函电》[M].北京：对外经济贸易大学出版社，2009.

[11] 武振山.《国际贸易英文函电》[M].大连：东北财经大学出版社，2004.

[12] 许德金.《实操商务英语教程——函电》[M].北京：首都经济贸易大学出版社，2009.

[13] 仲鑫.《外贸函电》[M].北京：机械工业出版社，2006.

参考网址

http://wenku.baidu.com/view/373490c52cc58bd63186bd5b.html

http://www.bbs.transn.com

http://www.blog.hjenglish.com

http://www.blog.sina.com.cn

http://www.chengdulawyergary.com

http://www.chinafanyi.com

http://www.chinadaily.com.cn

http://www.class.wtojob.com/practice_220.shtml

http://www.dict.cn/

http://www.dict.veduchina.com

http://www.dict.hjenglish.com

http://www.ecocn.org

http://www.en.bab.la

http://www.en.yeeyan.com

http://www.eng.chinaue.com

http://www.ftchinese.com

http://www.gmsw.sunbo.net/show.php?xname=5I58211

http://www.google.com/imghp?hl=en&tab=wi

http://www.huihua.iciba.com

http://www.iciba.com

http://www.jukuu.com

http://www.1x1y.com.cn

http://www.nipic.com

http://www.p.wink.blog.163.com

http://www.pkurc.com

http://www.sl.iciba.com

http://www.source.mastvu.ah.cn

http://www.space.100e.com

http://www.onlinetest.chit.edu.tw

http://www.x5dj.com

http://www.221.232.138.206

图书在版编目（CIP）数据

新编实用英语写作. 下册 / 肖付良，高平，刘燕主编.—北京：中国人民大学出版社，2013.4
普通高等教育"十二五"高职高专规划教材
ISBN 978-7-300-17310-8

Ⅰ.①新…　Ⅱ.①肖…　②高…　③刘…　Ⅲ.①英语–写作–高等职业教育–教材　Ⅳ.①H315

中国版本图书馆 CIP 数据核字（2013）第 063983 号

普通高等教育"十二五"高职高专规划教材
新编实用英语写作（下册）
主　　编　肖付良　高　平　刘　燕
副主编　曹淑萍　姚　娟
编　委　罗凌萍　赵熹妮　胡雁群　黄　珍　龚文锋　谢　丹
Xinbian Shiyong Yingyu Xiezuo (Xia Ce)

出版发行	中国人民大学出版社		
社　　址	北京中关村大街31号	邮政编码	100080
电　　话	010–62511242（总编室）	010–62511398（质管部）	
	010–82501766（邮购部）	010–62514148（门市部）	
	010–62515195（发行公司）	010–62515275（盗版举报）	
网　　址	http:// www. crup. com. cn		
	http:// www. ttrnet. com（人大教研网）		
经　　销	新华书店		
印　　刷	北京中印联印务有限公司		
规　　格	185 mm×260 mm　16开本	版　　次	2013年4月第1版
印　　张	12	印　　次	2013年4月第1次印刷
字　　数	248 000	定　　价	28.00元

中国人民大学出版社外语出版分社读者信息反馈表

尊敬的读者：

感谢您购买和使用中国人民大学出版社外语出版分社的 _____ 一书，我们希望通过这张小小的反馈卡来获得您更多的建议和意见，以改进我们的工作，加强我们双方的沟通和联系。我们期待着能为更多的读者提供更多的好书。

请您填妥下表后，寄回或传真回复我们，对您的支持我们不胜感激！

1. 您是从何种途径得知本书的：
   □书店　　　　□网上　　　　□报纸杂志　　　　□朋友推荐

2. 您为什么决定购买本书：
   □工作需要　　□学习参考　　□对本书主题感兴趣　　□随便翻翻

3. 您对本书内容的评价是：
   □很好　　　　□好　　　　□一般　　　　□差　　　　□很差

4. 您在阅读本书的过程中有没有发现明显的专业及编校错误，如果有，它们是：

   _____

   _____

   _____

5. 您对哪些专业的图书信息比较感兴趣：

   _____

   _____

   _____

6. 如果方便，请提供您的个人信息，以便于我们和您联系（您的个人资料我们将严格保密）：

   您供职的单位：_____

   您教授的课程（教师填写）：_____

   您的通信地址：_____

   您的电子邮箱：_____

请联系我们：黄婷　程子殊　于真妮　商希建　鞠方安

电话：010-62512737，62513265，62515037，62514974，62515576

传真：010-62514961

E-mail：huangt@crup.com.cn　　chengzsh@crup.com.cn　　yuzn@crup.com.cn
　　　　shandysxj@163.com　　jufa@crup.com.cn

通信地址：北京市海淀区中关村大街甲 59 号文化大厦 15 层　　邮编：100872

中国人民大学出版社外语出版分社